CONTENTS

CONTENTS

INTRODUCTION

To the teacher

This book follows the successful three-section format of our A level grammar *Aktion Grammatik!* and adapts it to the needs of the GCSE pupil. Each of the main chapters is divided into three sections: *Auf die Plätze!* explains the grammar point clearly in as simple English as possible; *Fertig?* offers reinforcement exercises on each point; and *Los!* provides a variety of oral and/or written activities in which the particular grammar point would occur naturally. As far as possible, the exercises and activities in the *Fertig?* and *Los!* sections are set in a context relevant to the Areas of Experience in the GCSE syllabuses. A lot of the vocabulary not found in the Foundation level lists provided by the Examination Boards is to be found in the *Glossar* at the end of each chapter.

Although the grammar explanation comes first, it is not intended that teaching should be 'grammar-led'; it is expected rather that pupils will have met most of the grammar points already in their main coursebook, and that this book will be used for consolidation, revision and reference. The self-check key at the end of the book for the *Fertig?* section will enable pupils to work at their own speed and check their own progress. The *Los!* section is there to provide enjoyment and to supplement the communicative activities of their coursebook, as well as helping to reinforce the grammar point in question. The exercises and activities are roughly graded in difficulty, with an **H** denoting those which are regarded as more suitable for Higher Level pupils only.

This book will provide pupils with the necessary grammatical support for their communicative abilities at both Foundation and Higher level, and for Higher level pupils, ease the transition from GCSE to A level.

To the pupil

This book is called *Grammatik Aktiv!* because grammar is an important element in understanding how a language works, and because (contrary to popular belief!) learning grammar can be fun! You've probably had plenty of practice at speaking, reading, listening and maybe writing, but you may still be a bit shaky on those verb tenses, adjective agreements and other points of grammar that you need to get the highest grade you can. This book is designed to help you tidy up your grammar. Each chapter is divided into three sections, representing 'Ready?', 'Steady?', 'Go!'. First, a section called *Auf die Plätze!*, in which each grammar point is explained in simple English, with plenty of examples. Then there are some exercises – *Fertig?* – to give you further practice – and a self-check key at the end of the book, so you can see for yourself what you have got right. Ask your teacher about what you didn't get right – and then have another go! Finally, there is a section of activities – *Los!* – where you can work some role-plays with your classmates or do some written work to further practise your grammar. You should be pretty confident after all that! Even then, you can carry on using the *Auf die Plätze!* section to look up anything you are still not sure about, and for your final revision. *Viel Glück!*

1

THIS IS HOW IT IS ...
structuring statements

 Auf die Plätze!

A simple German sentence works like this ...
Words generally work together to form **sentences**. The **order** of words or
structure of the sentence (**syntax**) gives it extra meaning (e.g. to emphasize a
certain section of the sentence).

Statements are sentences that **tell us** information, rather than asking questions.
In simple German sentences (main clause only), the **verb** must be the **second
element** or second idea.

Beispiel:

	1	2	3	4
	Man subject	***spricht*** **verb**	*Deutsch* object	*in Deutschland.* place
or:	*In Deutschland* place	***spricht*** **verb**	*man* subject	*Deutsch.* object
or even:	*Deutsch* object	***spricht*** **verb**	*man* subject	*in Deutschland.* place

 Fertig?

1 Alles in Ordnung?
Ordne die folgenden Wörter! Achtung: es gibt vielleicht mehr als eine richtige Lösung!

Put the following words in the correct order. Beware: there may be more than one correct version!

1. heiße   ich   Wagner   Richard
2. vierzehn   Jahre   bin   ich   alt
3. in   England   wir   wohnen
4. Geschwister   ich   keine   habe
5. in   der   Nähe   von   Bremen   Hamburg   liegt
6. Doppelhaus   haben   am   Stadtrand   wir   ein
7. Euro   kostet   zwei   das
8. Frühstück   um   acht   Uhr   esse   mein   ich
9. Klavier   spielt   gern   meine   Schwester
10. in   der   Stadtmitte   das   Rathaus   liegt

2 Richtig oder falsch?
Welche Sätze sind richtig und welche falsch? Abhaken oder ankreuzen! Kannst du die falschen Sätze verbessern?

Which sentences are correct and which are incorrect? Tick or cross! Can you correct the incorrect sentences?

1. Meine Schwester Monika heißt.
2. Sie ist fünfzehn Jahre alt.
3. Sie wohnt in der Schweiz.
4. Eine habe ich Katze.
5. In Österreich spricht man Deutsch.
6. Man spricht Deutsch in der Schweiz.
7. Ein Einfamilienhaus am Stadtrand wir haben.
8. Mein Mittagessen esse ich in der Kantine.
9. Spiele ich gern Geige.
10. Mein Lieblingsfach ist Deutsch.

 Los!

3 Bildertipps!
Erfinde zehn Sätze, die zu den folgenden Bildern passen!

Invent ten sentences to match the following pictures.

Beispiel:

Meine Maus heißt Käsi. 'My mouse is called Käsi'

4 *Wer ich bin, wo ich wohne, was ich mache…*
Schreibe zehn Sätze über dich selbst, deine Familie (und Haustiere), deinen Wohnort, dein Schulleben/dein Arbeitsleben, dein Privatleben!

Write ten statements about yourself, your family (and pets), the place where you live and what you do at work/school or at home.

5 *Richtig oder falsch?*
Ist dein Satzbau richtig? Kontrolliere mit einem Partner deine Sätze aus Übung 3!

Is your sentence structure correct? Check your sentences from Exercise 3 with a partner.

6 *Schnipsel, Schnipsel auf dem Tisch …*
Mache einen Satz aus diesem Gemisch! Nimm wieder deine Sätze aus Übung 3! Schneide dann die einzelnen Wörter aus. Aus dem Durcheinander musst du bzw. muss dein Partner eine richtige Aussage bilden!

Make a sentence out of a word-jumble! Use your sentences from Exercise 3 again. Cut each sentence out separately and then cut out each individual word. From the jumbled pile, you or your partner must form a correct sentence!

7 *Richtig oder falsch?*
Schreibe (eventuell mit deinem Computer) die zehn Sätze aus Übung 4! Kontrolliere später im Unterricht die Sätze deines Partners!

Write (or word-process) your ten sentences from Exercise 4. Perhaps later you could check your partner's work in class.

GLOSSAR

in der Nähe von…	near
ein Doppelhaus (n.)	a semi-detached house
ein Einfamilienhaus (n.)	a detached house
Klavier (n.) *spielen*	to play the piano
Geige (f.) *spielen*	to play the violin

2

WHAT ABOUT A QUESTION?
structuring questions

 **Auf die Plätze!**

How do you ask a question in German?
A German **question** is clearly different from a statement because:

■ the verb begins the sentence, or...

■ the sentence begins with a clear question word.

Beispiele:

> **Verb** begins the sentence

Hast du Geschwister?

Do you have brothers or sisters?

Wie viele Geschwister hast du?

How many brothers and sisters do you have?

> A **question word** begins the sentence

The most common question words are:

■ *Wie?*
Wie geht's deiner Schwester?
Wie ist deine Schwester?

How? What ... like?
How is your sister?
What's your sister **like**?

■ *Was?*
Was trinkst du zum Frühstück?

What?
What do you drink at breakfast?

■ *Was für ...?*
Was für Haustiere hast du?

What sort of ...?
What sort of pets do you have?

■ *Wo?*
Wo wohnst du?

Where?
Where do you live?

■ *Wann?*
Wann hast du Kunst?

When?
When do you have art (lessons)?

■ **(a)** *Wie viel(e) …?*
Wie viel Taschengeld bekommst du?

How much/how many …?
How much pocket money do you get?

Wie viele Bücher hast du?

How many books do you have?

(b) *Um wie viel Uhr …?*
Um wie viel Uhr stehst du auf?

At what time …?
At what time do you get up?

■ *Welcher/welche/welches?*
Welches ist dein Lieblingsfach?

Which?
Which is your favourite subject?

■ *Warum?*
Warum hast du keine Hausaufgaben gemacht?

Why?
Why don't you have any homework?

 Pass auf!

You can also use the **interrogative pronoun**, *wer*, to introduce questions (see above). *Wer* declines using the same endings as the masculine singular relative pronoun (see Chapter 26):

Nominative	*wer*	who
Accusative	*wen*	who(m)
Genitive	*wessen*	whose
Dative	*wem*	whom

Beispiel:

Wer bist du?   Who are you?

Wen siehst du da?   Who(m) do you see there?

Von wem hast du das Buch?   From whom do you have that book?

The genitive from *wessen* is usually avoided if possible as it sounds very formal, so:

Wessen Buch hast du?   Whose book do you have?

would be more easily expressed as:

Wem gehört das Buch?   Who does that book belong to?

Fertig?

1 Ein Interview. Lückentexte!
Fülle folgende Lücken mit Hilfe der oben angegebenen Fragewörter aus!

Fill in the following gaps with the correct question word taken from the list above.

1. … heißt du?
2. … Uhr ist es?
3. … geht's dir?
4. … Käse ist das?
5. … spielst du Tischtennis?
6. … Popgruppe hörst du am liebsten?
7. … hat keine Hausaufgaben?
8. … kostet das?
9. … kommt man am besten zur Stadtmitte?
10. … beginnt deine Mittagspause?

2 Mischmasch
Bring die Wörter in die richtige Reihenfolge!

Rewrite the following questions in the correct sequence!

1. Haustiere hast du?
2. Du in der Stadtmitte wohnst?
3. Weit von hier das ist?
4. Du isst zum Abendessen was?
5. Man kann fahren direkt?
6. Wiederholen bitte Sie das wollen?
7. Haus kannst beschreiben du dein?
8. Deutsch wir haben jetzt?
9. Ihr heute Hausaufgaben habt auf?
10. Alle seid fertig ihr?

3 Wie heißt die Frage?
Schreibe für folgende Antworten jeweils eine passende Frage!

For each of the following answers, write a suitable question.

1. …?   Ja, ich habe einen Bruder und eine Schwester.
2. …?   Nein, ich wohne in der Schweiz!
3. …?   Mein Lieblingsfach ist Sport.
4. …?   Das kostet €2,20.
5. …?   Das liegt in Nordwestdeutschland.

Los!

4 Zwanzig Fragen!
Schreibe zwanzig Fragen auf, wobei jede Frage anders beginnt!

Write out twenty questions, making sure that each question begins differently.

5 Los! Schreibe!
Schreibe einen Brief an deinen neuen Brieffreund! Stell ihm bzw. ihr so viele Fragen wie möglich! Für jede Frage, die du stellst, musst du auch eine treffende Antwort geben. Schreibe jetzt weiter!

Write a letter to your new pen friend. Ask him/her as many questions as possible. For each question that you ask, you must also give the relevant answer for yourself. Now write on!

Beispiel:

> Cardiff, den 2. März 2001
>
> Lieber _____,
>
> Wie geht's? Mir geht's gut. Hast du Geschwister? Ich habe keine Geschwister: ich bin Einzelkind! ...

GLOSSAR

Haustiere (pl.)	pets
wiederholen	to repeat
wollen	to want
fertig	finished, ready
Geschwister (pl.)	brothers and sisters

3

DO AS I SAY!
imperatives

 **Auf die Plätze!**

What is an imperative?
An imperative is an **order**, a **command** or an **instruction**.

1 Forming the imperative
When you order people to do something, in German they must know **two** things:

■ **WHAT you want them to do (the verb).**
   In commands (**an imperative**) this always **begins** the sentence.

■ **Exactly WHO you are ordering.**
   (See also Verb Forms: the Present Tense. Chapters 15–17.)
   In German there are **three** words meaning '**you**':

   1. *du* – for **one** person you know well, **informally**, e.g. a friend.
   2. *ihr* – for **more than one** person you know well, **informally**.
   3. *Sie* – for **one or more** people you treat more **formally** (e.g. a stranger, an older, respected person, or teacher!).

2 Using the imperative
The verb takes **the ending** which suits:

■ *du* form
   Take the *-(e)st* ending off the *du* form of the present tense. If there is an umlaut, remove it. Add an exclamation mark!

   Strictly, the *du-* form imperative of weak verbs should take an *-e* ending. This is often 'clipped':

   Beispiel: *Arbeite doch weiter!*

   BUT: *Kopier in dein Heft! Sag mir alles!*

10

Beispiele:

geben	*– du gibst*	**Gib** *mir deine Telefonnummer!*
schlafen	*– du schläfst*	**Schlaf** *gut!*
kommen	*– du kommst*	**Komm** *mit ins Kino!*

■ *ihr* **form**

Simply take the *ihr* form of the present tense, **without** mentioning the word *ihr*.
Add an exclamation mark!

Beispiele:

grüßen	*– ihr grüßt*	**Grüßt** *euch, Jungs!*
fahren	*– ihr fahrt*	**Fahrt** *mit uns ins Kino!*
sich setzen	*– ihr setzt euch*	**Setzt** *euch!*

■ *Sie* **form**

Simply take the *Sie* form of the verb. You must add the subject, *Sie*. Add an
exclamation mark!

Beispiele:

kommen	**– Sie kommen**	*Frau Fischer! Kommen Sie bitte mit!*
sich setzen	**– Sie setzen** *sich*	*Guten Tag! Setzen Sie sich, bitte!*
geben	**– Sie geben**	*Geben Sie mir Ihre Adresse!*

 Toller Tipp!

Let's go!
You can encourage or 'exhort' your friend(s) to do something with you by
using the *wir* form of the imperative, as in the English form 'Let's/Let us…':

Take the *wir* form.
Add *wir*.
Add an exclamation mark!

Beispiele:

gehen	*– wir gehen*	*Gehen wir ins Kino!*
nehmen	*– wir nehmen*	*Nehmen wir die U-Bahn!*
warten	*– wir warten*	*Warten wir mal!*

Pass auf !

Nicht vergessen!

In public notices or announcements which address (an) unknown reader(s) or audience, German simplifies the command:

Take the **infinitive** form.
Place it at the end of the imperative phrase.
Add an exclamation mark!

Beispiel:

rauchen	*Nicht rauchen!*
fahren	*Schritt fahren!*
halten	*Bei Rot, halten!*

 # Fertig?

1 Ordnung muss sein!
Bring die Wörter in die richtige Reihenfolge auf!

Write the following commands in the correct word order.

1. zu hört gut!
2. dein Heft mir zeig!
3. die Lücken aus füllt!
4. vor Text den lies!
5. auf Hausaufgaben die schreibt!
6. die Frage Sie bitte wiederholen!
7. jetzt Gruppen in arbeitet!
8. deinem stelle Fragen Partner!
9. langsamer bitte Sie sprechen!
10. Verspätung entschuldigen meine bitte Sie!

2 Bildertipps!
Schreibe die zehn in Übung 1 angegebenen Befehle neben das passende Bild!

Now write out the ten commands given in Exercise 1, opposite the picture cues which match them!

A

B

C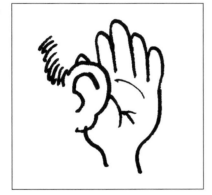

D

E

F

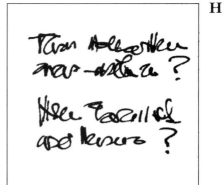

H 3 Was passt wozu?

Schreibe die Befehle aus der unten angegebenen Liste (a–j) auf, die zu folgenden Fragen (1–10) passen!

Write out the orders given in the list below (a–j) that best match the following questions (1–10).

1. Entschuldigung. Wie komme ich am besten zum Rathaus?
2. Kann ich Ihnen helfen?
3. Susi, wo kommt das Besteck hin?
4. Hallo, Thomas. Wie kommen wir zum Klassenzimmer?
5. Entschuldigung. Wie funktioniert dieses Telefon?
6. Also, Martin, kannst du mir helfen?
7. Ist der Campingplatz weit von hier?
8. Herr Müller. Wie schreiben wir diese Hausaufgaben?
9. Wo ist unser Bus?
10. Wie bekomme ich bitte eine Telefonnummer in England?

a. Ja, zwei Kilometer. Nehmen Sie die Straßenbahn Nummer 5!
b. Folgt mir!
c. Leg die Messer und Gabeln auf den Tisch!
d. Gehen Sie hier geradeaus bis zum Marktplatz! Da steht es.
e. Wählen Sie erstmal null, null, vier, vier und dann die Vorwahlnummer!
f. Heben Sie erstmal den Hörer ab!
g. Ja, geben Sie mir ein Kilo Kartoffeln!
h. Schaut mal! Da drüben steht er.
i. Füllt die Lücken aus!
j. Ja, sicher. Gib mir die Hand!

 ## Los!

4 Selbstkontrolle oder Partnerkontrolle?
Arbeite jetzt alleine oder mit einem Partner! Deck die Sätze auf der rechten Seite von Übung 2 Bildertipps zu, damit nur die Bilder erscheinen! Mit Hilfe der Bilder musst du die richtigen Befehle laut vorlesen.

With or without a partner, cover the sentences written on the right of Exercise 2 *Bildertipps*, so that only the pictures are showing. With the help of the pictures, read out the correct commands.

5 Mischmasch!
Man schreibt alle Sätze aus Übung 3 auf Karten und schneidet dann die einzelnen Wörter aus. Man legt alle Wörter in Unordnung auf den Tisch. Dann versucht man (alleine oder in Gruppen), richtige Befehle so schnell wie möglich zu 'sammeln'. Kleb sie auf Papier!

Cut up the individual words, copied onto card from the sentences in Exercise 3. Jumble them up on a table. Alone or in groups, collect words, one by one, and put them into meaningful commands. Stick them on some paper.

6 Wegweiser
Übe Befehle im Klassenunterricht mit deinem Partner in einem Dialog oder schreibe selber solche Dialoge wie im Beispiel!

Practise giving commands to a partner in class, or write a dialogue using commands as in the example:

Beispiel:

A Entschuldigen Sie, wie komme ich am besten zum Bahnhof?
B Gehen Sie hier links! Nehmen Sie die nächste Straße rechts!

7 *Wie kommst du zu mir?*

Dein Briefpartner besucht dich in zwei Wochen und kommt mit dem Zug/bzw. mit dem Bus. Zeichne zu Hause einen Plan von deiner Stadt bzw. deinem Dorf! Schreibe deinem deutschen Briefpartner einen Brief! Wie kommt er bzw. sie zu Fuß vom (Bus-) Bahnhof zu deinem Haus?

Your pen pal is visiting you in two weeks, arriving by train or bus. At home, draw a map of your town or village. Write a letter to your pen pal. How will he/she get from the (bus) station in your town/village to your house, on foot?

GLOSSAR

Jungs!	lads (colloquial)
zeigen	to show
Fragen stellen	to ask questions
das Besteck	cutlery
das Messer	knife
schauen	to look
sicher	certain(ly)
zuhören	to listen
aufschreiben	to write down
meine Verspätung	my late arrival
folgen	to follow
die Gabel	fork
die Vorwahlnummer	STD code
der Hörer	the receiver
Bei Rot, halten!	Stop at red light!
Schritt fahren!	Drive dead slow!

4

PERSON, PLACE OR THING?
nouns

 **Auf die Plätze!**

What is a noun?
A noun identifies a **person**, **place** or **thing**.

Beispiele:

Person	Place	Thing
Herr (m.) Schmidt	*der Bodensee (m.)*	*der Bus (m.)*
Frau (f.) Müller	*die Stadtmitte (f.)*	*die Schule (f.)*
das Mädchen (n.)	*Deutschland (n.)*	*das Wetter (n.)*
die Deutschen (pl.)	*die Vereinigten Staaten (pl.)*	*die Postkarten (pl.)*

1 Spelling
All German nouns begin with a **capital letter**!

Nouns have a **particular gender** form (*der, die, das*), according to whether they are **masculine (m.)**, **feminine (f.)** or **neuter (n.)**. Their form generally changes in the **plural (pl.)** – *die*. It is always best to learn the appropriate **definite article** (*der, die, das, die*) as you learn each noun. Thus, a noun listed in the dictionary as: '*Pass* (m.), *Pässe* (a) passport, (b) (mountain) pass', is clearly a **noun** (capital letter), **masculine** (m) and its **plural** form takes an **umlaut** (*-ä-*), so it is best learnt aloud as: ***der Pass, die Pässe***.

You will notice that the word meaning 'a(n)' also changes to suit a **masculine** word, (***ein Mann***), a **feminine** word (***eine Frau***) or a **neuter** word (***ein Mädchen***).

More will be explained about articles in the next two chapters.

2 Learning gender through endings

German has a clear pattern of typical endings which may help you to learn the gender of nouns.

a Generally masculine

■ **Male titles or roles**: *der Vat**er**, der Präsid**ent**, (der) Herr, Doktor …*

■ **Male jobs or activities**: *der Lehr**er**, der Busfahr**er**, der Kelln**er** …*

■ **Days, months, seasons**: *der Tag, Sonn**tag**, Diens**tag**, der Geburts**tag**, der Wint**er**, der Somm**er**, der Herbst, Oktob**er**, Dezemb**er**, Februar*

■ **Makes of car**: *dieser Mercedes, dein Volkswagen …*

■ **Most nouns ending in**: *-er*

> see above, and *der Comput**er**, der Taschenrechn**er** …*

This ending generally describes a **job or activity**.

b Generally feminine

■ **Female roles or titles**: *meine Mutter, Tant**e** Ulrik**e**, deine Schwester, eine Dam**e**, (die) Frau …*

■ **Female jobs or activities, ending in -in**: *die Lehrer**in**, die Kellner**in**, die Präsident**in** …*

■ **Most nouns with the following endings**:

-e	see above, plus: *meine Schul**e**, diese Seit**e**, eine Stund**e***
-ei	*die Bäcker**ei**, die Konditor**ei**, die Wäscher**ei***
-heit	*die Ein**heit**, meine Krank**heit**, die Gesund**heit***
-ie	*die Droger**ie**, Biolog**ie**, meine Famil**ie***
-ik	*die Bundesrepubl**ik**, die Informat**ik**, die Grammat**ik***
-keit	*meine Dankbar**keit**, deine Freundlich**keit**, keine Schwierig**keit***
-schaft	*die Land**schaft**, die Gesell**schaft**, deine Freund**schaft***
-tät	*die Universi**tät**, die Puber**tät**, meine Identi**tät***
-tion	*diese Informa**tion**, die Revolu**tion**, eine Na**tion***
-ung	*die Buchhandl**ung**, deine Verbesser**ung**, meine Verspät**ung***

c Generally neuter

■ **Note that 'things' in German are not just neuter, but can be equally masculine or feminine (see above).**

■ Equally nouns referring to some people can be neuter in gender: *das Mädchen, das Kind, dieses Fräulein, das Opfer.*

■ **Neuter endings include nouns ending in:**

-chen   *das Mäd**chen**, das Bröt**chen**, ein Päck**chen** …*

-um   *das Dat**um**, das Muse**um**, das Gymnasi**um** …*

■ **Nouns formed from infinitives, ending in *-en* are neuter:**

*das Ess**en**, das Pferderenn**en**, Ihr Schreib**en** …*

3 Why does gender matter?

For some words their **meaning** depends on their gender!

der See (z.B. *der Bodensee*) **lake** (e.g. Lake Constance),	**BUT**	*die* See (z.B. *die Ostsee*) **sea** (e.g. the Baltic)
der Kunde **customer**	**BUT**	*die* -kunde, z.B. *Erdkunde, Wirtschaftskunde* **study of**… (e.g. geography, economics)
der Leiter **manager**	**BUT**	*die* Leiter **ladder**
das Band (z.B. *das Tonband, das Gummiband*) audio **tape**, rubber **band**	**BUT**	*die* Band (z.B. *die Jazzband*) **group** (e.g. jazz band), and even *der* **Band** **volume** of a book

4 Compound Nouns

German often puts together long combinations of two or more nouns: *die Buch**handlung**, das Sport**waren**geschäft, der Boden**see**.*

The gender (*der, die, das*) of these nouns is the gender of their **final part**:

die Handlung	*die Buch**handlung***
das Rennen	*das Pferde**rennen***
der See	*der Boden**see***
das Land	*Deutsch**land**, Eng**land***
das Reich	*Öster**reich**, Frank**reich***

5 Plural Forms

We must also tell whether something is **singular** (*eine Schwester, ein Moment, eine Idee*), or **plural** (*drei Schwester**n**, einige Moment**e**, ein paar Idee**n***).

Grammatik Aktiv!

Where German 'borrows' a word directly from English (or French), it also borrows our typical '-s' plural ending:

ein Auto	*zwei Autos*
eine Rockband	*zwei Rockbands*
dieses Hotel	*alle Hotels*

But, German has typical plural forms of its own:

a Typically masculine

■ **add just an *umlaut*:**

ein Großvater	*zwei Großväter*
ein Bruder	*drei Brüder*

■ **add an *umlaut* + -*e*:**

ein Stuhl	*vier Stühle*
ein Sohn	*zwei Söhne*

■ **add just -*e*:**

der Tisch	*alle Tische*
ein Bleistift	*viele Bleistifte*

b Typically feminine

■ **add -*(e)n*:**

eine Kusine	*viele Kusinen*
eine Schwester	*zwei Schwestern*
eine Uhr	*zwei Uhren.*

■ **Note:** nouns ending in -*in* take a plural ending in -*innen*:

meine Lehrerin	*alle Lehrerinnen*
eine Studentin	*alle Studentinnen*

■ **add an *umlaut* (+ -*e*):**

eine Großmutter	*zwei Großmütter*
eine Hand	*beide Hände*
eine Nacht	*vier Nächte*

c Typically neuter

■ add an *umlaut* + *-er*:

    ein Buch   *zwei Büch*er
    ein Haus   *zwei Häus*er

■ **no change for neuter nouns which already have an** *umlaut*:

    *das M*ädchen   *die M*ädchen
    *dieses Fr*äulein   *viele Fr*äulein

Toller Tipp!

An umlaut can only be written above the 3 vowels, *a: ä*, *o: ö*, and *u: ü*.

6 Cases

German has four cases (see Chapters 10–14) affecting the form of *der*, *die*, *das*, etc.
(see p.22 for a full list of the forms of the articles).
Nouns are either:

■ in the **nominative** case, if they are the **subject** of an action.   (*der Mann*)
■ in the **accusative** case, as the **direct object** of an action.   (*den Mann*)
■ in the **genitive** case, where **possession 'of'** something is involved.   (*des Mannes*)
■ in the **dative** case, as the **indirect object** of an action.   (*dem Mann*)

7 Endings

Nouns take a particular ending:

■ in the **plural** form, generally see above
■ in the **dative plural** form, always: add *-n* to the plural
■ in the **genitive** case, if they are **masculine or neuter**: add *-(e)s* to the singular
■ in the **accusative**, **genitive and dative**, **singular or plural**, if they belong to a
    small group of weak nouns (see next page).

Toller Tipp!

Some adjectives can be used as nouns. Simply capitalise the first letter and
add the correct adjectival endings (see Chapter 28)
    eg.   *der Große*   the big one
        zwei Neue   2 new people/newcomers
        ein Deutscher   a German person

The table below may help to simplify their pattern of endings:

SINGULAR

	Masculine	Feminine	Neuter
Nominative	*der Vater*	*die Maschine*	*das Kind*
Accusative	*den Vater*	*die Maschine*	*das Kind*
Genitive	*des Vaters*	*der Maschine*	*des Kind(e)s*
Dative	*dem Vater*	*der Maschine*	*dem Kind*

PLURAL

	Masculine	Feminine	Neuter
Nominative	*die Väter*	*die Maschinen*	*die Kinder*
Accusative	*die Väter*	*die Maschinen*	*die Kinder*
Genitive	*der Väter*	*der Maschinen*	*der Kinder*
Dative	*den Vätern*	*den Maschinen*	*den Kindern*

8 Weak nouns

This small group of nouns is always masculine. Some of these are very common, others much less so. Amongst the most common are:

der Affe	monkey, ape	*der Automat*	(vending) machine
der Bauer	farmer, peasant	*der Beamte*	official, civil servant
der Buchstabe	letter (of the alphabet)	*der Franzose*	Frenchman
der Herr	gentleman	*der Kunde*	customer
der Junge	boy	*der Mensch*	person, human
der Nachbar	neighbour (m.)	*der Name*	name
der Neffe	nephew	*der Präsident*	president (m.)
der Student	student (m.)	*der Wille*	will (power)

Not only the article, but also the **noun** itself takes **endings**, as shown below:

SINGULAR

Nominative	*der Herr*	*der Student*	*der Beamte*
Accusative	*den Herrn*	*den Studenten*	*den Beamten*
Genitive	*des Herrn*	*des Studenten*	*des Beamten*
Dative	*dem Herrn*	*dem Studenten*	*dem Beamten*

PLURAL

Nominative	*die Herren*	*die Studenten*	*die Beamten*
Accusative	*die Herren*	*die Studenten*	*die Beamten*
Genitive	*der Herren*	*der Studenten*	*der Beamten*
Dative	*den Herren*	*den Studenten*	*den Beamten*

Fertig?

1 Wo steht das Substantiv?
Unterstreiche die Substantive in folgenden Sätzen!

Underline the nouns in the following sentences.

1. Mein Vater heißt Rainer. Er ist Leiter der Volksbank.
2. Hast du eine Schwester oder einen Bruder?
3. Wann hast du Geburtstag? Im Dezember oder im März?
4. Mein Onkel hat ein neues Auto; es ist ein Audi … oder ist es ein Mercedes?
5. Der Bodensee liegt zwischen der Schweiz, Österreich und Deutschland.

2 Maskulinum oder …? Singular oder …?
Ordne folgende Substantive in der richtigen Spalte: Maskulinum, Femininum, Neutrum!
Singular oder Plural? Wer 'Auf die Plätze' gelesen hat, braucht kein Wörterbuch!

Put the following nouns in the correct column: deciding whether they are
masculine, feminine, neuter, singular or plural! If you have read *'Auf die Plätze'*, you
won't need a dictionary!

Beispiel:

a. Mein Vater heißt Rainer. Er hat ein deutsches Auto, aber meine Mutter fährt
immer Renaults: diese Autos kommen aus Frankreich.

	SINGULAR (s.)			PLURAL (pl.)
	Maskulin (m.)	Feminin (f.)	Neutrum (n.)	
1. Beispiel	Vater	Mutter	Auto	Renaults
	Rainer		Frankreich	Autos

b. 'Hast du Geschwister?'
'Ja, ich habe einen Bruder und zwei Schwestern. Meine ältere Schwester heißt
Sophie. Sie wohnt in Schottland. Sie hat einen Sohn und eine Tochter.'

c. 'Was lernst du in der Schule?'
'Ich habe Erdkunde und Informatik zweimal in der Woche: am Mittwoch und am Donnerstag. Diese Fächer sind meine Lieblingsfächer!'

d. 'Was machst du im Sommer?'
'Ich arbeite im Juli und August als Kellnerin in einem Hotel. Die besten Hotels sind in Österreich. Und du?'

e. Mein Bruder, meine Kusine und ich fahren an die Nordsee zum Surfen oder vielleicht zum Bodensee. In der Schweiz kaufen wir neue Uhren und sehen das Pferderennen in St. Moritz!

f. Die Busse fahren am Montag mit den Schülern zur Schule.

g. Das Wetter interessiert die Engländer mehr als die Franzosen.

h. Frau Müller hat Herrn Schmidts Postkarten aus den Vereinigten Staaten total vergessen!

3 So ein Mist!
Deine deutsche Brieffreundin hat dir einen schönen Brief auf ihrem Computer geschrieben, aber ihr Drucker hat die Endungen der Substantive schlecht gedruckt! Kannst du die Lücken eventuell ergänzen?

Your German pen friend has written you a nice letter on her computer, but her printer has missed off most of the endings of the nouns! Can you fill in the gaps where necessary?

```
                                    Berl…, den 20. Dezemb…
Lieber Brieffreund!

  Dein Brud… John hat mir einen schönen Br… auf Deut…
geschrieben. Meine Famil… findet das sehr interessant!

Ich habe zwei Schwest…: sie heißen Ulrik… und Sabin…
Hast du Geschwist…? Hast du auch Haustier…? Ich habe
eine Katz… und sechs Goldfisch…

Was machst du im Wint…? Wir fahren mit zwei Auto… nach
Öster… Dort besuchen wir meine beiden Tanten Brigitte
und Irmgard. Sie haben zwei schöne Hotel… in der Nähe
von Salzb…

Leider habe ich immer viele Hausaufgabe… und ich muss
meine Büch… in den Urlaub mitnehmen! Ich schicke dir aber
zwei Postkarte… aus den Alp…

            Alles Gute wünscht dir
                deine Elk…
```

Los!

4 Was ist das?

Vokabeln aus dem Deutschunterricht. Versuch das Spiel mit einem Partner oder, noch besser, in einer Gruppe! 'A' versteckt etwas (was er selber auf Deutsch beschreiben kann) unter seinem Pullover oder in einer Tasche. 'B' fragt 'Was ist das?' unter seinem Pullover bzw. in einer Tasche. 'A' muss den Gegenstand beschreiben. Wenn 'B' ihn richtig identifiziert, bekommt er/sie einen Punkt. Einen zweiten Punkt bekommt er, wenn er den treffenden Artikel (der, die, das) richtig identifiziert.

Vocabulary from your German lesson. Try this with a partner or, better still, in a group. Person 'A' hides something (which he or she can describe in German) under their jumper or in a bag. Person 'B' asks: *Was ist das?* Person 'A' must describe the object they are hiding. If Person 'B' correctly identifies the object, he/she wins a point, plus another point if the correct article (*der, die, das*) is used.

Beispiel:

B   Was ist das?

A   Das ist ein Stück Obst. Der ist grün und knackig.

       Die Runde geht dann weiter, indem der Nächste jetzt die Frage stellt; *'Was ist das?'*, usw.

5 *Reiseziele*

Nimm dein Wörterbuch bzw. einen deutschsprachigen Atlas! Schreibe die Namen der Länder in vier Spalten auf (wie bei Übung 2)! Was bemerkst du dabei?

Using your German dictionary or a German atlas, list countries in four columns (as in Exercise 2). What do you notice?

6 *Urlaubsfantasie*

Schreibe zwölf Sätze! Jeder Satz beginnt mit einem verschiedenen Monat und endet mit einem verschiedenen Land als Reiseziel. Gute Reise!

Write twelve sentences. Each sentence should begin with a different month and end with a different country you are visiting. Enjoy your trip!

Beispiel:
Im *Januar* besuche ich *die Schweiz.*

GLOSSAR	
der Leiter (m.)	the manager
der Bodensee (m.)	Lake Constance
das Pferderennen (n.)	horse-racing
Erdkunde (f.)	geography
Informatik (f.)	information technology
so ein Mist! (m.)	what a mess!

5

THE ..., THIS ... AND THAT...!
the definite article

 ## Auf die Plätze!

What is the definite article?

In Chapter 4 you see how the **endings** of **nouns** often tell you whether they are masculine, feminine or neuter, singular or plural. To make it even clearer, **before** each noun you will often find a short **article** e.g. *der*, *die* or *das*, which also gives the reader or listener some more information. In English, the **definite** article is simply our word 'the ...'.

Beispiel:

> The **definite** article

Das Kaninchen heißt 'Bugsy'.   **The** rabbit is called 'Bugsy'.

We use the **definite** article *das* to refer to **the** particular rabbit in question.

1 The four cases and the definite article

Chapters 10–14 will further explain how important **cases** are in German. Briefly consider the following:

a Nominative

The **nominative** case (*der*, *die*, *das*, *die*) is used for the person or thing which does the action (the **subject** of the action):

*Was kostet **der** Kassettenrekorder?*   (masculine, singular)
*Wohin fährt **die** Straßenbahn?*   (feminine, singular)
***Das** Kaninchen heißt 'Bugsy'.*   (neuter, singular)
***Die** Gummibärchen kosten € 5.*   (plural)

b Accusative

The **accusative** case tells us that the person or thing described is the **direct object** of the action:

subject		**direct object: accusative**		
Ich	*kaufe*	***den** Kassettenrekord**er**.*		(masculine)
Mein Onkel	*nimmt*	***die** Straßen**bahn**.*		(feminine)
Hast du		***das** Kanin**chen***	*gekauft ?*	(neuter)
Wollen wir		***die** Würstchen*	*kaufen?*	(plural)

c Genitive

The **genitive** case describes possession, or the connection '**of**' something/someone to another:

*Die Farbe **des** Kassettenrekorder**s*** finde ich toll!*	(masculine)
*Die Fahne **der** Bundesrepublik ist schwarz, rot, gold.*	(feminine)
*Wie heißt die Adresse **des** Museum**s***?*	(neuter)
*Der Preis **der** Würstchen ist zu hoch!*	(plural)

 **Pass auf!**

Masculine and **neuter** NOUNS also take the **-s** ending* of their article (*des*) in the genitive singular.

d Dative

The **dative** case refers to a person, place or thing **to** which/whom, **with** which/whom, **from** which/whom we do something (the **indirect object** of the action). It is also necessary after certain prepositions ‡ (see Chapters 12 and 13).

*Gib **dem** Deutschlehrer deine Kassette!*
*Kommst du aus‡ **der** Bundesrepublik?*
*Von‡ **dem** Museum habe ich einen Prospekt bekommen.*
*Mit‡ **den** Würstchen habe ich Pommes Frites gegessen.*

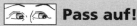 **Pass auf!**

All **nouns** in the **dative plural** must also take the **-n** ending found in the **article**:
*Ich spreche nicht sehr oft mit de**n** Lehrer**n** aber mit de**n** anderen Schüler**n** spreche ich gern!*

2 Tables
a The definite article
To help you to remember the correct forms of the **definite article**, here is a table:

der, die, das, die (the)

	SINGULAR			PLURAL
	Masculine	**Feminine**	**Neuter**	
Nominative	*der*	*die*	*das*	*die*
Accusative	*den*	*die*	*das*	*die*
Genitive	*des*	*der*	*des*	*der*
Dative	*dem*	*der*	*dem*	*den*

b dieser, jeder, solcher, jener and welcher
Since the **same** set of endings as *der, die, das...* is also taken by *dieser* (this, these), *jeder* (each/every), *solcher* (such), *jener* (that, those), and *welcher...?* (which...?), you might like to learn these now, too!

dieser (this/these)

	SINGULAR			PLURAL
	Masculine	**Feminine**	**Neuter**	
Nominative	*dieser*	*diese*	*dieses*	*diese*
Accusative	*diesen*	*diese*	*dieses*	*diese*
Genitive	*dieses*	*dieser*	*dieses*	*dieser*
Dative	*diesem*	*dieser*	*diesem*	*diesen*

jeder (each/every) (NB: plural = *alle*)

	SINGULAR			PLURAL
	Masculine	**Feminine**	**Neuter**	
Nominative	*jeder*	*jede*	*jedes*	*alle*
Accusative	*jeden*	*jede*	*jedes*	*alle*
Genitive	*jedes*	*jeder*	*jedes*	*aller*
Dative	*jedem*	*jeder*	*jedem*	*allen*

solcher (such)

	SINGULAR			PLURAL
	Masculine	**Feminine**	**Neuter**	
Nominative	*solch*er	*solch*e	*solch*es	*solch*e
Accusative	*solch*en	*solch*e	*solch*es	*solch*e
Genitive	*solch*es	*solch*er	*solch*es	*solch*er
Dative	*solch*em	*solch*er	*solch*em	*solch*en

 Pass auf!

Since *jeder* means 'each', it cannot have a plural form. Use **alle** in the plural.
Beispiel:

jede Woche	each/every week
alle zwei Wochen	every two weeks

jener (that/those)

	SINGULAR			PLURAL
	Masculine	**Feminine**	**Neuter**	
Nominative	*jen*er	*jen*e	*jen*es	*jen*e
Accusative	*jen*en	*jen*e	*jen*es	*jen*e
Genitive	*jen*es	*jen*er	*jen*es	*jen*er
Dative	*jen*em	*jen*er	*jen*em	*jen*en

Welcher...? (which...?) NB: also often an abbreviation of *irgendwelcher* (some (or other))

	SINGULAR			PLURAL
	Masculine	**Feminine**	**Neuter**	
Nominative	*welch*er	*welch*e	*welch*es	*welch*e
Accusative	*welch*en	*welch*e	*welch*es	*welch*e
Genitive	*welch*es	*welch*er	*welch*es	*welch*er
Dative	*welch*em	*welch*er	*welch*em	*welch*en

Toller Tipp!

See Chapter 37: Appendix II for a quick glance at all the grammatical tables needed at this level.

Fertig?

1 Der, die oder das?
Fülle folgende Lücken mit dem bestimmten Artikel der, die, das, die usw. aus!

Fill in the following gaps using the definite article *der, die, das, die* etc.

a. Nominativ
1. Wie heißt ... Präsident?
2. Was kostet ... Mercedes?
3. Was kostet ... Auto?
4. Wie heißt ... Schwester von deinem Partner?
5. Wie viel kosten ... Bonbons?

b. Akkusativ
6. Mein Vater kauft ... Volkswagen des Monats!
7. Willst du ... Postkarte kaufen?
8. Wir besuchen ... Haus meines Partners.
9. Ja, ich nehme ... fünf Kassetten zu einer Mark!
10. Bringst du bitte ... neuen Bücher in die Bibliothek?

c. Genitiv
11. Der Name ... neuen Deutschlehrers ist Depp!
12. Die Farbe ... Tischlampe ist rosa.
13. Wie heißt die Frau ... Deutschlehrers?
14. Wie ist die Farbe ... neuen 50-Euroscheine?
15. Das Datum ... nächsten Klassenarbeit ist der erste April!

d. Dativ

16. Wie komme ich am besten zu … Bahnhof?
17. Isst du dein Mittagessen in … Schulkantine?
18. Ich kaufe meine Kassetten in … Einkaufszentrum.
19. Gibst du bitte … Deutschlehrerin meine Hausaufgaben?
20. Du fährst hier geradeaus und an … Ampel musst du rechts abbiegen.

2 Der, die, das … auf jeden Fall?

Fülle folgende Lücken mit dem bestimmten Artikel – je nach der grammatischen Rolle des folgenden Substantivs – aus!

Fill in the following gaps with the definite article, according to the grammatical role of the following noun.

1. 'Entschuldigung! Wo liegt hier d… Rathaus (n.), bitte?'
   'Nehmen Sie d… zweite Straße (f.) rechts. An d… Ampel (f.) biegen Sie links ein. D… Rathaus (n.) liegt auf d… rechten Seite (f.) d… Doms (m.).'
2. In d… Stadtmitte (f.) steht ein alter Dom. D… Dom stammt aus d… zwölften Jahrhundert (n.) und liegt hinter d… Marktplatz (m.). D… Namen (m.) d… Doms habe ich aber vergessen!
3. D… schnellsten Autos (pl.) kommen aus Deutschland, d… schönsten (pl.) kommen aus Italien, aber d… beste Auto (n.) d… Welt (f.)? Mit d… Auto fährt immer James Bond!
4. D… Preise (pl.) d… besten Weinsorten (pl.) sind immer hoch! D… Name (m.) d… schönsten Weins (m.) meines Lebens? D… Namen sage ich dir nicht!

⊞ 3 Der, die, das? Dieser? Jener? Jeder? Solcher? Welcher …?

Fülle folgende Lücken mit der passenden Form der obrigen Wörter aus!

Fill in the following gaps with the appropriate form chosen from the above words.

1. … Heft (n.) brauchen wir für die Hausaufgaben? … oder …?
2. … Woche (f.) fahre ich normalerweise mit … Bahn (f.) zur Arbeit, aber … Woche fahre ich mit … Bus (m.).
3. … deutsche Grammatik (f.) finde ich schwer! Aber … deutschen Vokabeln (pl.) sind einfach: … Wörter (pl.) wie 'Fisch', 'Haus' und 'Mann' sind wie … englischen Vokabeln (pl.)!
4. Sag mal! … Hose (f.) gefällt dir am besten? … hier in grün oder … da drüben in schwarz?
5. … Samstag (m.) kaufe ich … Magazine (pl.) wie 'Tophits' oder 'Teenager' in … Supermarkt (m.).

Los!

4 Versteckt! (Kim's game)

Spielt in einer Gruppe von 5 bzw. 6 Personen oder in ganzen Mannschaften!
Die Klasse sammelt und identifiziert eine Gruppe von Gegenständen, z.B. das Heft, das Buch, der Radiergummi, das Lineal, die Tasche.

Ein Spieler, 'A', bzw. eine Mannschaft, 'A', verlässt das Zimmer.

Die anderen, 'B', verstecken die Gegenstände.

Das Spiel beginnt, wenn die Mannschaft (bzw. der Spieler) zurückkommt.

Play in a group of five or six people, or in a whole team.
The class collects and identifies a group of objects, e.g. exercise book, book, rubber, ruler, bag.

Player 'A' or team 'A' leaves the room.

The others, 'B', hide objects.

The game begins when the team (or player) comes back.

Beispiel:

Mannschaft bzw. Spieler 'A' fragt:	'Wo ist der Apfel?'
	(Nominativform)
'B' muss antworten:	'Ich habe den Apfel in der Ecke unter einem blauen Buch versteckt.'
	(Akkusativform)

'A' bekommt den Punkt, wenn er einen Gegenstand findet.
'B' bekommt einen Punkt, wenn 'A' den Gegenstand nicht findet.

⊞ 5 Nominativ, Akkusativ, Genitiv, Dativ?

Lies einen Zeitungsartikel oder eine Touristenbroschüre! Identifiziere alle Substantive!
Schreibe sie mit Hilfe eines Wörterbuchs nach folgendem Beispiel auf!

Read a German newspaper article or tourist brochure. Identify all the nouns. Write them down in a box, as shown below, using a dictionary to help you.

Beispiel:

Köln – die Stadtmitte

Der Dom liegt in der Nähe des Hauptbahnhofs am Rheinufer. Man
erreicht die Stadtmitte am besten mit der S-Bahn...

	Maskulinum	Femininum	Neutrum	Plural
Nominativ	der Dom			
Akkusativ		die Stadtmitte		
Genitiv	des Hauptbahnhofs			
Dativ		(in) der Nähe (mit) der S-Bahn	(an) dem Rheinufer	

GLOSSAR

die Tischlampe	table lamp
die Klassenarbeit	test
die Ampel	traffic lights
der Hauptbahnhof	main (train) station
die S-Bahn	tram, urban railway
der 50-Euroschein	50 Euro note
das Einkaufszentrum	shopping centre
der Dom	cathedral
das Rheinufer	bank of the River Rhine

6

MY IDEA, NO IDEA!
the indefinite article

 **Auf die Plätze!**

What is the indefinite article?
In Chapter 5 you see how the German definite article, *der*, *die* or *das* etc. is the
English equivalent of the simple English definite article 'the'!

Now we will take a look at the equivalent of the English 'a' or 'an'. This is called the
indefinite article: *ein, eine, ein*.

Beispiel:

The **indefinite** article

*Hast du **ein** Kaninchen?*   Do you have **a** rabbit?

*Nein, ich habe **kein** Kaninchen.*   No, I don't have **a (any)** rabbit.

The **indefinite** article,
expressing the **negative**

The **indefinite article** describes a subject or object which is not particular.

1 The four cases and the indefinite article
Chapters 10–14 will further explain how important **cases** are in German.

Briefly consider the following:

a Nominative

The **nominative** case (*ein, eine, ein*) applies to the **person** or **thing** which *does* the action (the **subject** of the action):

*Was kostet **ein** Stadtplan?*	(masculine, singular)
*Was für **eine** Kassette ist das?*	(feminine, singular)
***Ein** Taxi kommt gleich!*	(neuter, singular)

 Toller Tipp!

When describing somebody's job, status or role, German drops *the indefinite article:

Meine Mutter ist *Hausfrau.
Ich bin *Vegetarier.

b Accusative

The **accusative** case (*ein**en**, eine, ein*) tells us that the person or thing is the **direct object** of the action:

		Subject		Direct Object: Accusative	
Hast	*du*			*ein**en** Stadtplan?*	(masculine)
	Ich	*kaufe*		*ein**e** neue Kassette.*	(feminine)
Holen	*Sie*	*bitte*		***ein** Taxi!*	(neuter)

c Genitive

The **genitive** case describes the possession or connection '**of**' something/someone to another:

*Der Preis ein**es** Kinobesuchs[†] ist zu hoch!*
*Die Arbeit ein**er** Krankenschwester ist schwer!*
*Wie ist die Farbe ein**es** Londoner Taxis[†]?*

 **Pass auf!**

Masculine and **neuter nouns** also take the **-s** ending[†] of their article (*eines*) in the genitive singular.

d Dative

The **dative** case refers to a person, place or thing **to** which/whom, **with** which/whom or **from** which/whom we do something (the **indirect object** of an action). It is also necessary after certain prepositions[‡] (see Chapters 12 and 13).

*Ich spiele oft mit‡ ein**em** Schulfreund.*   (masculine, dative)
*Ich bekam gestern diese Postkarte von‡ ein**er** Brieffreundin.*   (feminine, dative)
*Mein Austauschpartner studiert an‡ ein**em** Gymnasium.*   (neuter, dative)

2 Tables
a The indefinite article
To help you to learn and to remember the correct forms of the indefinite article and the possessive pronouns listed below, here are some tables:

	SINGULAR			**PLURAL**
	Masculine	**Feminine**	**Neuter**	
Nominative	*ein*	*ein**e***	*ein*	–
Accusative	*ein**en***	*ein**e***	*ein*	–
Genitive	*ein**es***	*ein**er***	*ein**es***	–
Dative	*ein**em***	*ein**er***	*ein**em***	–

Jemand (someone) and *niemand* (no-one) take the same endings as the masculine singular indefinite article.

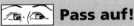 **Pass auf!**

There is, of course, **no plural form of** *ein* ('one'), but the following have the same pattern of endings and these **do** have plural forms:

kein-	not a(n)/no	***sein-***	its
mein-	my	***unser-***	our
dein-	your (singular, informal)	***euer-***	your (plural, informal)
sein-	his	***Ihr-***	your (singular/plural:formal)
ihr-	her	***ihr-***	their

---

b Kein, mein, dein, sein and ihr

	SINGULAR			**PLURAL**
	Masculine	**Feminine**	**Neuter**	
Nominative	*kein*	*kein**e***	*kein*	*kein**e***
Accusative	*kein**en***	*kein**e***	*kein*	*kein**e***
Genitive	*kein**es***	*kein**er***	*kein**es***	*kein**er***
Dative	*kein**em***	*kein**er***	*kein**em***	*kein**en***

The singular possessives **mein-, dein-, sein-** and **ihr-** follow exactly the same pattern, thus:

	SINGULAR			PLURAL
	Masculine	**Feminine**	**Neuter**	
Nominative	*mein*	*mein*e	*mein*	*mein*e
Accusative	*dein*en	*dein*e	*dein*	*dein*e
Genitive	*sein*es	*sein*er	*sein*es	*sein*er
Dative	*ihr*em	*ihr*er	*ihr*em	*ihr*en

c Plural possessives

The **plural possessives** follow the same pattern and may be tabulated together, thus:

	SINGULAR			PLURAL
	Masculine	**Feminine**	**Neuter**	
Nominative	*unser*	*unser*e	*unser*	*unser*e
Accusative	*Ihr*en	*Ihr*e	*Ihr*	*Ihr*e
Genitive	*eur*es	*eur*er	*eur*es	*eur*er
Dative	*ihr*em	*ihr*er	*ihr*em	*ihr*en

Toller Tipp!

See Chapter 37: Appendix II for a quick glance at all the grammatical tables needed at this level.

Fertig?

1 Lückentexte!

Fülle folgende Lücken mit ein- oder kein- aus!

Now fill in the following gaps, using *ein-* or *kein-*.

a. Nominativ

1. … Mercedes ist teuerer als … Volkswagen!
2. Ist hier … Drogerie in der Nähe?
3. Wie viel kostet … Brötchen, bitte?
4. Ich habe Durst und … Kellner kommt!
5. Hier steht … Datum auf dem Brief! Wann ist er angekommen?

b. Akkusativ

6. Wir haben … Kaninchen.
7. Wo finde ich hier bitte … Konditorei?
8. Ich habe nur … Bruder, ich habe … Schwester!
9. Kaufst du mir bitte … neue Kassette?
10. Was kostet … Briefmarke? Ich habe … Ahnung!

c. Genitiv

11. Der Preis … CD ist teurer geworden!
12. Die langen Arbeitsstunden … Lehrer … hätte ich nicht gern!
13. Der Hunger … Kaninchen … hat kein Ende!
14. Die wichtigste Stadt … Bundesland … ist die Landeshauptstadt.
15. … Tag … möchte ich Wien besuchen!

d. Dativ

16. Ich gehe jedes Wochenende mit … Freundin in die Disko.
17. Nein, wir wohnen in … Einfamilienhaus!
18. Mein Austauschpartner kommt aus … Stadt in der Nordschweiz.
19. Wie heißt das englische Äquivalent von … Bundesland?
20. Das Schlimmste an … Porsche ist sein Benzinkonsum!

2 Ein Artikel oder kein Artikel?

Fülle folgende Lücken mit der passenden Form des unbestimmten Artikels bzw. des Possessivums aus! Vorsicht bei Berufen!

Fill in the following gaps with the appropriate indefinite article or possessive pronoun. Be careful with job descriptions!

1
A. Wie heißt … Schwester (f.)?
B. … Name (m.) ist Kerstin. Und wie heißt … Bruder (m.)?
A. … Name ist Heiko.

2
A. Habt ihr … Hund (m.)?
B. Ja, … Hund heißt Benno. Und ihr habt … Katze (f.), nicht wahr? Wie ist … Name?
A. … Katze heißt Mizi. Das ist doch die Katze von … Schwester. Ich habe leider … Haustiere (pl.): ich bin allergisch gegen Haustiere!

3

A. Sieh dir das Foto an! Also du, sind das … Eltern (pl.)?

B. Nein, … Eltern sind jünger! Guck mal hier! Hier ist … Mutter. Sie ist … Sekretärin in der Firma … Vaters (m.).

4

Guten Abend! Willkommen in … Hotel (n.)! Wir wünschen Ihnen … schönen Aufenthalt (m.)! Wie war … Reise (f.)? Wollen Sie hier bitte … Namen (m.) eintragen? In … Hotelzimmer (n.) finden Sie … Infokarte (f.) neben dem Telefon, aber Sie finden … Aschenbecher (m.). In … Hotelzimmer ist das Rauchen nicht erlaubt! Sie sind … Nichtraucher (m.), ja?

5

A. In den letzten Sommerferien habe ich mit vielen Freunden … Schloss (n.) im Rheinland besucht. … Besuch (m.) hat uns aber nicht so gut gefallen!

B. Wieso, denn? Habt ihr … Geld (n.) verloren?

A. Nein, aber jemand hat … Fotoapparate (pl.) gestohlen und den Rest … Besuchs haben wir auf einer Polizeiwache verbracht! Du, ich möchte niemals … Polizist (m.) werden!

 # Los!

3 Einfach Klasse! Kein Problem!

Intensive Übung von dein-/mein-, ein/kein-, dein-/kein- usw. In Paaren lässt sich das Spiel stufenweise aufbauen und erweitern!

Intensive oral practice and repetition of *dein-/mein-, ein/kein-, dein-/kein-* etc. In pairs you can build up and continue expanding the game.

Beispiel:

Erste Phase:

A.	Wie heißt *dein* Bruder?	(Nominativ)
B.	*Mein* Bruder heißt …	(Nominativ)

Zweite Phase:

    A.   Wie heißt *dein* Bruder?   (Nominativ)

    B.   Ich habe *kein*en Bruder!   (Akkusativ, neg.)

Dritte Phase:

    A.   Haben Sie *eine* Briefmarke?   (Akkusativ, Singular)

    B.   Nein, ich habe *kein*e Briefmarken! (Akkusativ, Plural, neg.)

Denk dir weitere Fragen mit dem Nominativ, Akkusativ, Genitiv und Dativ aus. Benutze auch Singular- und Pluralformen.

⊞ 4 Mein Haus, meine Familie, mein Zimmer

Schreibe einen Brief (am besten mit Foto), wo du dein Haus, deine Familie, dein Zimmer beschreibst! Versuch, alle unbestimmten Artikel bzw. Possessive und die Substantive durch eine bestimmte Farbe zu identifizieren, z.B. Maskulinum: blau, Femininum: rot, Neutrum: grün, Plural: orange! Identifiziere auch, wo möglich, den Kasus (Nom./Akk./Gen./Dat.) in Klammern!

Write a letter, preferably with a photo, describing your house, your family, your room. Try to identify the nouns and their indefinite articles or possessives with a colour code, e.g. masculine: blue, feminine: red, neuter: green, plural: orange. If possible, also identify the case (nom./acc./gen./dat.) in brackets.

Beispiel:

    Ich wohne in einem Doppelhaus (grün: Dat. Neut.). Mein Haus (grün: Nom. Neut.) hat eine Garage (rot: Akk. Fem.) und einen Garten (blau: Akk. Mask.). Die Farbe meiner Haustür (rot: Gen. Fem.) ist braun …

⊞ 5 Genitiv: genial! Bunte Sprache!

Intensive Übung und Wiederholung von Genitivformen in Paaren!
Stell deinem Partner eine Frage mit der Genitivform des unbestimmten Artikels!
Dein Partner muss mit dem passenden Possessivum in der Genitivform darauf antworten.
Kein Partner? *Dann schreibe Frage und Antwort als Dialog einfach auf!*

Intensive practice and repetition of genitive forms of the indefinite article, in pairs. Ask your partner a question in the genitive form of the indefinite article. Your partner must answer using the appropriate form of the possessive.
No partner? Then simply write up the question and answer in dialogue form!

Grammatik Aktiv!

Beispiel:

Erste Phase:

A fragt:	Welche Farbe haben die Augen *deiner* Schwester?
B antwortet:	Die Augen *meiner* Schwester sind grün.
B fragt:	Und welche Farbe haben die Augen *deiner* Schwester?
A antwortet:	Die Augen *meiner* Schwester sind blau.

Zweite Phase:

A fragt:	Welche Farbe hat das Auto *deiner* Schwester?
B antwortet:	Das Auto *meiner* Schwester ist schwarz.
B fragt:	Und welche Farbe hat das Auto *deines* Bruders?
A antwortet:	Das Auto *meines* Bruders ist rot.
A fragt:	Und welche Farbe hat das Auto *deiner* Eltern?
	…usw.

GLOSSAR

der Kinobesuch	a visit to the cinema
das Schlimmste	the worst thing
das Gymnasium	grammar school
leider	unfortunately
guck mal!	just look!
der Aschenbecher	ashtray
die Polizeiwache	police station
die Krankenschwester	nurse
der Benzinkonsum	petrol consumption
der Kellner	waiter
der Aufenthalt	stay, residence
nicht erlaubt	not permitted
gestohlen	stolen

7

COUNTING
numbers

 **Auf die Plätze!**

1, 2, 3, 4, 5 ...
You won't go far without numbers! Buying a train ticket, asking for a departure time, counting your money and getting into the right carriage on the right platform are all typical examples of when you need numbers. Add to that dates, addresses, postcodes, telephone numbers, distances, directions, timetables, and above all, shopping, and you'll see that few moments will go by without you needing a number!

Numbers are often reeled off at speed in conversation, on the radio, T.V., telephone, over a loudspeaker or at a ticket desk, so you need to **learn them thoroughly** and to **practice** them **aloud regularly**!

1 Let's count! Cardinal numbers
a Numbers 1 to 30

1	ein**s**	11	elf	21	**ein**undzwanzig
2	**zw**ei (zwo)	12	z**w**ölf	22	zweiundzwanzig
3	drei	13	dreizehn	23	dreiundzwanzig
4	**v**ier	14	vierzehn	24	vierundzwanzig
5	f**ü**nf	15	fünfzehn	25	fünfundzwanzig
6	se**ch**s	16	sechzehn	26	sechsundzwanzig
7	sieben	17	siebzehn	27	siebenundzwanzig
8	a**ch**t	18	achtzehn	28	achtundzwanzig
9	neun	19	neunzehn	29	neunundzwanzig
10	**z**ehn	20	z**w**anzig	30	drei**ß**ig

Toller Tipp!

Challenging sounds have been <u>underlined</u> above to help you to concentrate on perfecting the numbers.

The sound *z* (= *-ts-*) in endings like **_dreizehn_** and *-ss-* in **_dreißig_** (= *-ssich-*) make the key difference between thir-**teen** and thir-**ty**.

Practice them aloud!

 Pass auf!

Some points to watch:

1. *Ein*s is used only when counting, e.g. **_eins_**, *zwei*, *drei*…
   In longer numbers, the **-s** disappears, e.g. **ein***undzwanzig*.
   In front of a noun, *ein-* must take the appropriate endings
   (see Chapter 6):

   > *eine Schwester*

   But: *Ich bin mit **ein***undzwanzig *Jahren zum ersten Mal in die Kneipe gegangen!*

2. The form **zwo** helps to dinguish *zwei* from *drei* on the radio, T.V. or telephone.

b Numbers 30 to 100

Large, compound numbers are written as one word and, as in the old English nursery rhyme: 'four-and-twenty blackbirds…', the units precede the tens:

30	dreißig	40	vierzig
31	**ein**unddreißig	50	fünfzig
32	**zwei**unddreißig	60	sechzig
33	**drei**unddreißig	70	siebzig
34	**vier**unddreißig	80	achtzig
35	**fünf**unddreißig	90	neunzig
36	**sechs**unddreißig	100	(ein) hundert
37	**sieben**unddreißig		
38	**acht**unddreißig		
39	**neun**unddreißig		

c Numbers 100 to 199

100 (ein)hundert	115 (ein)hundertfünfzehn
101 (ein)hundert(und)eins	116 (ein)hundertsechzehn
102 (ein)hundertzwei	117 (ein)hundertsiebzehn
103 (ein)hundertdrei	118 (ein)hundertachtzehn
104 (ein)hundertvier	119 (ein)hundertneunzehn
105 (ein)hundertfünf	120 (ein)hundertzwanzig
106 (ein)hundertsechs	121 (ein)hunderteinundzwanzig
107 (ein)hundertsieben	130 (ein)hundertdreißig
108 (ein)hundertacht	140 (ein)hundertvierzig
109 (ein)hundertneun	150 (ein)hundertfünfzig
110 (ein)hundertzehn	160 (ein)hundertsechzig
111 (ein)hundertelf	170 (ein)hundertsiebzig
112 (ein)hundertzwölf	180 (ein)hundertachtzig
113 (ein)hundertdreizehn	190 (ein)hundertneunzig
114 (ein)hundertvierzehn	199 (ein)hundertneunundneunzig

You continue to form the numbers following the patterns shown above.

d Numbers 200 and beyond...

200 zweihundert	700 siebenhundert
201 zweihundert(und)eins	800 achthundert
202 zweihundertzwei	900 neunhundert
222 zweihundertzweiundzwanzig	999 neunhundertneunundneunzig
300 dreihundert	1 000 (ein)tausend
400 vierhundert	1 001 (ein)tausend(und)eins
500 fünfhundert	8 888 achttausendachthundertachtundachtzig
600 sechshundert	1 000 000 **eine Million**

The word *eine Million(-en)* is treated as a noun with a **capital** initial letter and is **separated** from the remaining **unbroken string of numbers,** e.g.(inflation in 1920's Germany):

*Neunzehnhundertsechsundzwanzig bekam mein Großvater neun **Millionen** achtzigtausend Mark pro Woche!*

or:

9 876 541: *neun Millionen achthundertsechsundsiebzigtausendfünfhunderteinundvierzig*

Pass auf!

Some more points to watch:

1. **Number-combinations**
   Dates are written as one word:
   1963   *neunzehnhundertdreiundsechzig*
   (more about dates in Chapter 8)

   When saying number combinations, such as *Lottozahlen* (national lottery numbers), **telephone numbers** and **postcodes** aloud, numbers are often given in **pairs**, but sometimes **singly**, for clarity's sake:

   Die Postleitzahl für Köln ist: **fünfzigtausend Köln**   *(50000 Köln)*

   Meine Postleitzahl in Hamburg ist: **zwei, eins, null, sieben, sieben**
   (21077 Hamburg)

   Die Telefonnummer der Schule ist **sechsundsiebzig, einundzwanzig** *und die Vorwahlnummer ist* **null, vier, eins, sieben, drei**   *(0 41 73) 76 21*

2. **Time:** Like most continental Europeans, Germans naturally use the 24-hour clock:
   Die Schule ist um **dreizehn** *Uhr fünfunddreißig aus.*   **13.35**/1.35 **p.m.**
   (see Chapter 8 for more on 'time')

3. **Prices** must clearly identify (even with a pause) the division between *Mark* and *Pfennig*; *Schilling* and *Groschen*; and *Franken* and *Rappen*:
   Dieser Pullover kostet **fünfundneunzig** *(Mark),* **neunundneunzig** *(Pfennig).*   *(95,99 DM)*

4. German **postcodes** are five-figure numbers, written **before** the name of the town or village, whereas the **house number** is placed **after** the street name:
   Meine Adresse ist:
   Bahnhofstraße **5a**,
   53117 *Bonn-Buschdorf.*

5. Germans use a **comma** where the British use a decimal point!:
   1 000 000 = eine Million   1 000 = (ein)tausend
   3,95 DM = drei (Mark), fünfundneunzig (Pfennig)
   Mein Durchschnitt in Deutsch ist drei **Komma** *vier (3,4)*
   my average grade is 3.4
   (see also *Schulnoten*, Chapter 9)

2 Wie kalkuliert man das?

Doing sums

addieren:	1 + 11 = 12	eins **plus** elf ist zwölf
subtrahieren:	0 – 6 = –6	null **weniger/minus** sechs ist **minus** sechs
multiplizieren:	3 × 13 = 39	drei **mal** dreizehn macht neununddreißig
teilen:	40 ÷ 5 = 8	vierzig **durch** fünf gibt acht

There are three alternatives in German for equals, these are shown above: *ist, macht* or *gibt* (never use *sind, machen* or *geben*).

3 Fractions

Halb… e.g. ein halber Liter Milch = a half
Anderhalb/**einein**halb… e.g. anderthalb/eineinhalb Kilo Käse = one and a half

4 Alles in Ordnung!

Putting things in order: ordinal numbers

Ordinal numbers are used to show what position or order something is in. Just as with cardinal numbers, German **ordinal** numbers are quite like their English cousins.

1st	**erste**	11th	elf**te**	21st	**ein**undzwanzig**ste**
2nd	zwei**te**	12th	zwölf**te**	22nd	**zwei**undzwanzig**ste**
3rd	**dritte**	13th	dreizehn**te**	23rd	**drei**undzwanzig**ste**
4th	vier**te**	14th	vierzehn**te**	24th	**vier**undzwanzig**ste**
5th	fünf**te**	15th	fünfzehn**te**	25th	**fünf**undzwanzig**ste**
6th	sechs**te**	16th	sechzehn**te**	26th	**sechs**undzwanzig**ste**
7th	**siebte**	17th	siebzehn**te**	27th	**sieben**undzwanzig**ste**
8th	ach**te**	18th	achtzehn**te**	28th	**acht**undzwanzig**ste**
9th	neun**te**	19th	neunzehn**te**	29th	**neun**undzwanzig**ste**
10th	zehn**te**	20th	zwanzig**ste**	30th	dreißig**ste**
				31st	**ein**unddreißig**ste**
					… usw.

Ordinal numbers are adjectives and therefore take **adjective endings** after **definite**, **indefinite articles** and *dieser*, *jede*, *meine*, *kein* etc. (see adjectival endings in Chapter 28).

> *Ich habe Geburtstag am neunzehnt**en** Januar.*
> *Ich wohne im fünft**en** Stock eines Wohnblocks.*
> *Du nimmst die zweit**e** Straße links, dann die fünft**e** Straße rechts.*

The good news is that you will easily learn these endings in the contexts in which you need them, as in the above examples.

 Pass auf!

Take special notice of the forms:

> *ers**te**, drit**te**, sieb**te***

Apart from these few exceptions, for the ordinal numbers 1st–19th, the **ending -*te*** is simply **added** to the (cardinal) number concerned.

For 20th and onwards the ending -***ste*** is added:

> *Gestern war der dreißig**ste** Dezember*
> *Heute haben wir den **ein**unddreißig**sten** Dezember*

– hence the use of this **accusative form** in letter headings.

> *Morgen ist mein **ein**undzwanzig**ster** Geburtstag!*

 Fertig?

1 Aufschreiben!
Wähl für jede Zahl (a–j) die passenden Worte (1–10). Schreibe sie anschließend aus!

For each number (a–j) choose the words which match (1–10). Now write them out.

a.	1,5kg	1.	eine Mark fünfundneunzig
b.	31	2.	meine Postleitzahl ist sechs, zwo, null, null.
c.	(0 26 51) 43 43	3.	ein Meter neunundfünfzig
d.	1,59m	4.	meine Vorwahlnummer ist null, zwei, sechs, fünf, eins
e.	1 500 000	5.	dreißig weniger eins
f.	30 + 1	6.	eine Million fünfhunderttausend
g.	30 – 1	7.	einunddreißig
h.	1,95 DM	8.	den dreizehnten Mai neunzehnhundertachtundneunzig
i.	13.05.98	9.	anderthalb Kilo
j.	CH-6200 Luzern	10.	dreißig plus eins

2 Alle Zahlen zählen

Fülle die Lücken mit Hilfe der unten angegebenen Ziffern aus! Jede Ziffer muss als Wort erscheinen.

Fill in the gaps using the numbers given below. Each number must appear as a word!

1. Im Dezember werde ich … Jahre alt.
2. Am … habe ich Geburtstag.
3. Mein Vater ist genau … Meter groß.
4. Und der Gewinner hat die Nummer …
5. Ich wohne in Gauting, Postweg …
6. Die Postleitzahl für Schwerin ist …
7. Der Kuli kostet … Mark …
8. Das Motorrad kostet … Mark.
9. Ich bin … geboren.
10. Das Päckchen ist … Kilo schwer.

1,5kg	1963	15	2,00m	DM 1.999	21b	15.07
19,90 DM		19063 Schwerin		Lottozahl: 19-06-03		

3 Schule, Noten, Zeugnis und Mathe!

Fülle die Lücken im folgenden Brief mit Hilfe der unten angegebenen Zahlen aus!

Fill in the gaps in the following account about school, using the numbers given below.

Plymouth, den ... März

Liebe(r) Ulli!

Ich bin ... Jahre alt. Nach dem deutschen Schulsystem bin ich in der ... Klasse. Meine Schule hat ... Schüler bzw. Schülerinnen im Alter von ... bis ... Jahren. Ich habe ... Stunden pro Tag: der Unterricht beginnt um ... und endet um ... . Mein Klassenzimmer für Deutsch liegt im ... Stock. Ich habe dieses Jahr gute Noten in Deutsch bekommen: eins, drei und zwei: also einen Durchschnitt von ... .

Deutsch ist mein Lieblingsfach!

Alles Gute wünscht dir
deine Sandra.

---

neun Uhr	ersten	zehnten	einunddreißigsten	achtzehn	elf	acht
achthundert	fünfzehn Uhr dreißig		zwei Komma null		sechzehn	

Los!

4 Lotto!

Schreibe die Lottozahlen der letzten vier Wochen auf! Jetzt kannst du:

a. *mit einem Partner im Unterricht üben. Der Partner hört die Lottozahlen und muss sie als Zahl aufschreiben;*
b. *diese Zahlen deinem deutschsprachigen Briefpartner schicken. Er soll dir die letzten Lottozahlen (als Worte) zurückschicken, damit das Spiel weitergeht.*

Write down the lottery numbers for the last four weeks in German words.
Now you can:

a. practice with your partner in class. Your partner listens to the lottery numbers and writes down the numerals;
b. send them to your German-speaking pen friend: he should then send back his most recent lottery numbers (in word form) and the game can continue.

5 *Wo ich wohne*

Du wohnst in einem Wohnblock am Stadtrand (z.B. von Alpendorf). Schreibe deinem Briefpartner einen Brief und zeichne einen Plan vom Wohnblock und von der Stadt (*Beispiel unten)! Erklär deinem Partner, wie er deine Wohnung findet! Tausch deinen Brief mit deinem Partner aus! Findet ihr beide die richtige Wohnung? Interessanter wird's, wenn du möglichst viele Ordinalzahlen verwendest.

You live in a block of flats on the outskirts of town. Write a letter to your pen pal, and in it draw a plan of the building and a map of the town (*example below). Explain to your partner how he gets to your flat. Exchange the letter with your partner. Can you both find the correct flat? It will be even more interesting if you use as many ordinal numbers as possible.

Beispiel:

> Vom Bahnhof nimmst du die … **te** Straße links und dann die … **te** Straße rechts. Ich wohne im … **ten** Stock im … **ten** Wohnblock rechts.

*Alpendorf

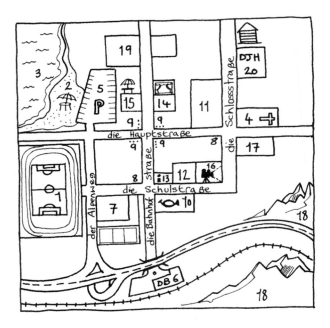

6 *Mein Stundenplan*

Zeichne deinen Stundenplan oder deinen Tagesablauf auf! Schreibe einem Briefpartner einen Brief, wo du beschreibst, was du machst, um wie viel Uhr, in welcher Stunde! Gib deinem Partner den Brief ohne die Zeichnung! Der Partner soll jetzt deinen Stundenplan bzw. deinen Tagesablauf richtig aufzeichnen!

Grammatik Aktiv!

Draw out your timetable or a plan of your daily routine. Write your pen pal a letter, in which you describe what you do, at what time or in which lesson. Give the letter to your partner without the drawing. He must then draw your timetable or routine plan correctly.

Beispiel:

London, den 1. April 2000

Liebe Jutta,

heute habe ich Geburtstag! Ich bin ... Jahre alt. Um ... Uhr gehe ich mit ... Freunden in die Disko. Wir werden dort ... Stunden lang tanzen und trinken, aber zuerst muss ich um ... Uhr in die Schule gehen. Meine erste Stunde beginnt um ... Uhr. Die Schule endet um ... Uhr und dann ...!

Alles Gute wünscht dir deine

Viola

P.S.
Schreib deine Telefonnummer in ganzen Worten auf! Ich kann deine deutschen Zahlen nicht lesen!

GLOSSAR

genau	exactly
mein Durchschnitt	my average grade (1–6)
die Kneipe	pub
nach	after, according to…
die Note	academic grade
zählen	to count
die Postleitzahl	postcode
die Vorwahlnummer	area code
das Klassenzimmer	classroom
das Lieblingsfach	favourite subject

8

WHEN, WHEN, WHEN?
times and dates

 Auf die Plätze!

1 Die Uhrzeit

Guten Morgen!   *Guten Tag!*   *Guten Abend!*
Wie spät ist es?   *Wie viel Uhr ist es?*   *Um wie viel Uhr fährt der Zug?*

Making reference to the **time** is a large part of our lives. Learning to tell the time as a youngster is a challenge in your native language, so **pay attention** in German!

1.
[01.00]

Es ist ein Uhr

2.
[19.00]

Es ist neunzehn Uhr
Es ist sieben Uhr abends

3.
[07.05]

Es ist sieben Uhr fünf
Es ist fünf nach sieben

4.
[07.20]

Es ist sieben Uhr zwanzig
Es ist zwanzig nach sieben

5.
[15.50]

Es ist fünfzehn Uhr fünfzig
Es ist zehn vor vier

6.
[15.55]

Es ist fünfzehn Uhr fünfundfünfzig
Es ist fünf Minuten vor vier

7.
[18.15]

Es ist achtzehn Uhr
fünfzehn
Es ist Viertel nach sechs

8.
[18.30]

Es ist achtzehn Uhr
dreißig
Es ist halb sieben

9.
[18.45]

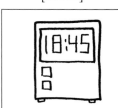

Es ist achtzehn Uhr
fünfundvierzig
Es ist Viertel vor sieben

10.
[12.00]

Es ist (zwölf Uhr)
Mittag

11.
[24.00]

Es ist (zwölf Uhr)
Mitternacht

12.
[00.10]

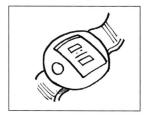

Es ist zehn nach
zwölf
Es ist null Uhr zehn

■ **In German, as in English, there are two ways to say the time:**

Es ist achtzehn Uhr fünfzehn	It is six fifteen
Es ist Viertel nach sechs	It is quarter past six

■ **When using the 12-hour clock German uses:**

Viertel nach …	a quarter past …
Viertel vor …	a quarter to …
halb …	half …

> 👀 **Pass auf!**
>
> Be **extra careful** when using *halb* – in German it means half way through the hour **to** … (not past as in English):
>
> | | |
> |---|---|
> | *Es ist halb zehn* | It is half past nine |
> | *Es ist neun Uhr dreißig* | It is nine thirty |

■ **When using the 24-hour clock, think of it like this:**

6.45 p.m. = 12 + 6.45 = *Es ist **achtzehn** Uhr fünfundvierzig*

■ **When referring to time:**   ***um***   means (precisely) 'at'

   gegen   means 'at about'

*Der Zug fährt **um** achtzehn Uhr zehn.*
The train leaves at (precisely) ten past six in the evening.

*Wir treffen uns dort **gegen** acht Uhr.*
We'll meet there at about eight o'clock.

■ **Remember that *Stunde* means the period of an hour**:

Es dauert eine Stunde.   It takes one hour.

and ***Uhr*** means o'clock (in the context of telling the time).

■ **If you do not want to be precise, you can use *manchmal* (sometimes) or *oft* (often).**

Ich gehe manchmal dorthin.   I go there sometimes.
Ich fahre oft mit dem Zug.   I often travel by train.

2 Die Tage der Woche
The days of the week are:

Montag	Monday	*Freitag*	Friday
Dienstag	Tuesday	*Samstag (Sonnabend)*	Saturday
Mittwoch	Wednesday	*Sonntag*	Sunday
Donnerstag	Thursday		

3 Dates (see Chapter 7, Ordinal Numbers)

■ **Days of the week are nouns and take a capital initial letter.**

■ **Time expressions in German are most commonly put into the accusative, including dates on letter headings. Note also the simple full stop which represents the ending of the ordinal number:**

den 1./2./3. März   1**st**/2**nd**/3**rd** March

■ **a precise day or date can be pinpointed by using *an* + *dem* = *am*... + dative ending:**

Wann fährst du das nächste Mal nach Düsseldorf?
*Nächste Woche **am Dienstag** fahre ich dorthin.*
Am drit**ten** Oktober mit dem Auto.

■ regular habit, on the other hand, is simply reflected in the genitive *-s* ending:

Wie oft spielt ihr hier Federball zusammen?
*Wir spielen hier mittwoch**s** und freitag**s** und immer um drei Uhr nachmittag**s**.*

4 Yesterday, today, tomorrow

Note also the following time expressions:

gestern	yesterday	*letzte **Nacht***	**late** last night
*morgen**	tomorrow	***vor**gestern*	the day **before yesterday**
letztes Jahr	last year	***über**morgen*	the day **after tomorrow**
nächste Woche	next week	***vor**letztes Jahr*	the year **before** last
*gestern **Abend***	last night/	***über**nächste Woche*	the week **after** next
	yesterday evening	**m***orgen** **früh**	tomorrow morning

(*avoiding the confusion between **m**orgen tomorrow, and **M**orgen morning!)

How long/how often?

Time expressions involving *haben* or a period of time require the accusative ending (written in bold):

*Welch**en** Tag/D**en** wie viel**ten** haben wir heute?*
*Heute haben wir Mittwoch, d**en** ersten Mai.*
***Wie lange** warst du auf Urlaub?*
*Wir waren ein**en** Tag/ein**e** Woche/ein**en** Monat lang in den Alpen.*
***Wie oft** fährst du nach Berlin?*
*Jed**en** Morgen/jed**en** Nachmittag/jed**en** Abend/jed**en** Freitag/jed**e** Woche/jed**en** Monat/jed**es** Jahr fahre ich dorthin.*

5 Die Monate und Jahreszeiten

Januar	*Februar*	*März*	*April*
Mai	*Juni*	*Juli (Julei)*	*August*
September	*Oktober*	*November*	*Dezember*

*der Frühling/**im** Frühling*	***im** März*
*der Sommer/**im** Sommer*	***im** Juli*
*der Herbst/**im** Herbst*	***im** Oktober*
*der Winter/**im** Winter*	***im** Dezember*

Pass auf!

1. In the list of months on the previous page, the vowel in bold shows you which syllable to **stress** when saying these aloud.

2. The prepositions (i) *um* and (ii) *am* precede (i) time on the clock and (ii) days/dates respectively. Months and seasons are preceded by the preposition *im...*

3. *Im Jahre 1989 fiel die Berliner Mauer/Im Oktober 1989 wurde Deutschland wieder eins.*
   but...*1961 wurde die Berliner Mauer gebaut.*

   i.e. **Years do not need the preposition *in*...** unless the noun *Jahr* precedes them.

6 Feiertage/Festtage!

Public holidays and celebrations:

zu Weihnachten	at Christmas
zu Ostern	at Easter
zu Pfingsten	at Whitsun

...but:

am zweiten Weihnachtstag	on Boxing Day
am Heiligen Abend	on Christmas Eve
zum Geburtstag	on my/your birthday...

 # Fertig?

1 Wie spät ist es jetzt in Wien?

Beispiel:

Los Angeles — New York — London — Wien

Grammatik Aktiv!

Schreibe jetzt die Antworten in vollen Sätzen auf oder übe sie mündlich mit einem Partner!

Write the answers out in full sentences or practise aloud with a partner.

1. In London ist es **dreiundzwanzig Uhr**: (a) wie spät ist es in Wien? (b) und in New York?
2. In London ist es **Mitternacht**: (a) wie viel Uhr ist es in New York? (b) und in Los Angeles?
3. In London ist es **Viertel vor elf**: (a) wie spät ist es in Los Angeles? (b) und in Wien?
4. In New York ist es **halb zwei** morgens: (a) wie spät ist es in Los Angeles? (b) und in London?
5. In New York ist es **zwanzig Uhr fünfunddreißig**: (a) wie spät ist es in Wien? (b) und in Los Angeles?

2 Den wie vielten haben wir heute?
Schreibe Tag und Datum in einem vollen Satz auf!

Write the day and date in words, in a complete sentence.

Beispiel:

Mo.12.12.   Heute haben wir Montag, den zwölften Dezember.

1. Mo.01.01
2. Mi.03.03
3. Do.31.05
4. Sa.12.10
5. Di. 28.02

3 Früher oder später …!
Verbinde folgende Daten mit den unten angegebenen Ereignissen!

Link the following dates with the events given below!

1. landete Wilhelm der Eroberer in Hastings.
2. fahre ich um acht Uhr abends in die Stadt.
3. landete Julius Cäsar in England.
4. ist Christus geboren!
5. bauten Daimler und Benz ihr erstes Auto!
6. gewann England die Fußballweltmeisterschaft in Wembley!
7. brach der zweite Weltkrieg aus.
8. beginnt das Neue Jahr.
9. ist es Mittag in Los Angeles.

a. Im Jahre 1939
b. Am ersten Januar
c. Ca.* 56 vor Christus
d. 1885
e. Sechsundfünfzig Jahre später
f. 1066
g. 1966
h. Neun Stunden später als in Wien
i. jeden Freitag

*ca. = circa: approx.

Los!

4 Schnipsel, Schnipsel auf dem Tisch …

Mach einen Satz aus diesem Gemisch! Schreibe alle Sätze aus Übung 3 (oben) auf!
Schneide dann die einzelnen Wörter aus. Aus dem Durcheinander musst du bzw. dein
Partner eine richtige Aussage bilden. (Siehe Kapitel 1. Los! Übung 6).

Make a sentence out of a muddle! Write down all the correct sentences from
Exercise 3 above. Cut each sentence into word-groups. From the muddle, you or
your partner must create a correct sentence. (see Chapter 1. *Los!* Exercise 6).

5 Und wann …?

Übe (mit deinem Partner) und schreibe den Dialog auf!

Practice the following dialogue (with your partner) and then write it down.

1. *Wann* hast du Geburtstag?
2. *Was für ein Wochentag* ist das, nächstes Jahr?
3. *An welchen Tagen* lernst du Deutsch?
4. *Um wieviel Uhr* isst du dein Frühstück?
5. *Wann* bist du geboren?

Erfinde 5 weitere Fragen und die Antworten dazu!

Create 5 more questions and answers!

Welches Paar kann das:

a. *am schnellsten (aufschreiben)?*
b. *am besten vor der Klasse spielen?*
c. *am interessantesten darstellen?*

Which pair can do this:

a. fastest?
b. best in front of the class?
c. in the most interesting way?

H 6 Datensuche

Lies einen Zeitungsartikel oder eine Touristenbroschüre, wo viele Tage, Zeiten und Daten
erscheinen! Schreibe die Sätze in voller Form auf!

Read a German newspaper article or tourist brochure, in which days, times and
dates frequently appear. Write out the sentences in German in full.

Beispiel:

Kunstgalerie. Mo, Sa, 10.00–15.00 geöffn.(25.12, 01.01. geschl.)

**Die Kunstgalerie ist montags und samstags
geöffnet, aber am fünfundzwanzigsten
Dezember und am ersten Januar ist sie geschlossen.**

⊞ 7 *Und wann..? Bist du sicher?*
Übe als Dialog oder informiere dich bei deinem (Brief-)Freund!

Practice as a dialogue or get information from your (pen)pal.

Beispiel:

A   Wann hast du Weihnachtsferien?
B   Also, Weihnachtsferien habe ich *am* 23. Dezember…
A   Bist du sicher?
B   Na, also *gegen den* 23. Dezember, aber vielleicht am 22. Dezember.
    Und du?

*Bilde weitere Fragen so, dass die Jahreszeiten, Feiertage, Ferien, Daten aus der Geschichte
und andere wichtige Zeitpunkte diskutiert werden!*

Make up more questions, in which you discuss important dates such as seasons,
holidays and historical dates.

Beispiele:

1. Wann beginnt der Frühling?
2. Um wie viel Uhr fährst du nach Hause?
3. In welchem Jahr fiel die Berliner Mauer?
4. Wann feiert man Karneval bzw. Fasching?

GLOSSAR

das Geschenk	present, gift
Christus	Christ
Jugendliche	adolescents
bauen	to build
Wilhelm der Eroberer	William the Conqueror
der Zweite Weltkrieg	the Second World War
die Kunstgalerie	art gallery

9

HOW BIG, HOW FAR?
quantities and measures

 Auf die Plätze!

1 Let's go metric
Trying to explain your height in **feet** and **inches** or buying food in ounces will get you nowhere in continental Europe, so practice at home and measure up to the metric reality! Consider:

Wie weit?

*Zehn **Millimeter** sind ein **Zentimeter**.*	10 **mm** = 1 **cm**
*Hundert Zentimeter sind **ein Meter**.*	100 cm = 1 **m**

Wie groß?

*Ich bin ein Meter achtzig **groß**.*	I am 1.80 metres **tall**.

Wie schnell?

Ich laufe die hundert Meter in 10,6 Sekunden!	I can run 100 m in 10.6 seconds!
*Mein Fahrrad fährt maximal 50 **Stundenkilometer**.*	My bike's top speed is **50 km/h.**

Wie weit?

*Tausend **Meter** sind ein **Kilometer**.*	1,000 **metres** = 1 **km**
*Berlin ist **ca.** 600 Kilometer von Bonn entfernt.*	Berlin is **approx.** 600 km from Bonn.

Wie viel Liter?

*Hundert **Zentiliter** sind **ein Liter**.*	100 **cl** = 1 **l**
***Dreißig Liter** bleifreies Benzin, bitte!*	30 l of unleaded petrol, please!
***Ein Liter** Milch, bitte!*	**1 litre** of milk, please.
***Ein halbes Liter** Olivenöl, bitte!*	**Half a litre** of olive oil, please!

Anderthalb Liter Wein.
Ein Glas (0,2 l) Weißwein, bitte!

One and a half litres of wine.
A glass of white wine, please.

Wie viel Gramm?

Tausend Milligramm sind ein Gramm.
1000 Gramm sind ein Kilo(gramm).
200 Gramm Wurst, bitte!
Ein Pfund Tomaten, bitte!

1,000 mg = 1 g
1,000 g = 1 kg
200 g (a quarter) of sausage, please.
A pound of tomatoes, please! (500 g)

Wie viel wiegst du?

Ich wiege 50 Kilo!
Dieses Päckchen wiegt eineinhalb Kilo.

How much do you weigh?
I weigh approx. 8 stone.
This parcel weighs **1.5 kg**.

Maße!

Was misst dieses Paket?
Wie groß ist es?
Wie lang ist es?
Wie breit ist es?
Und wie hoch ist der Eiffelturm?
Er ist dreihundertzwanzig Meter hoch!

What does this parcel **measure**?
How **high** is it?
How **long** is it?
How **wide** is it?
How **high** is the Eiffel Tower?
It is 320 m **high**.

Und das Wetter?

Wie warm ists?
28 Grad: schön warm!
Wie ist die Lufttemperatur?
Tiefstwerte: minus 6 Grad (Celsius).
Achtung: es folgt eine Sturmwarnung!

Windstärke 10 bis 12!

How **warm** is the water?
28 **degrees** (C): nice and warm!
What's the air-temperature like?
Minimum temperature: –6° **C**.
Attention: there follows a storm-warning
Force 10 to 12!

Pass auf!

1. After expressions of quantity, German uses no word for 'of':

   *ein Liter * Milch*   one litre *of milk

2. Kilo/Liter/Gramm/Meter etc. have no plural ending:

   zwei Meter   two metres
   fünfhundert Gramm   five hundred grammes

2 Schulnoten

One standard measure of which Germans are very keenly aware is their standard academic grading system (used for ages 6 to 20+):

1:	*eins*	*sehr gut*	very good	(A grade)
2:	*zwei*	*gut*	good	(B/B+)
3:	*drei*	*befriedigend*	pleasantly satisfactory	(B–/C+)
4:	*vier*	*ausreichend*	adequate	(C/C–)
5:	*fünf*	*mangelhaft*	patchy	(D grade)
6:	*sechs*	*ungenügend*	unsatisfactory	(E/U grade)

Mein Durchschnitt
Beispiel:

> *In Mathe hatte ich eine Zwei, eine Vier und eine Drei: mein Durchschnitt ist also drei!*
> In Maths I got a two, a four and a three, so my average grade is three (B-/C+).

 Pass auf!

Here *eine Zwei* is a grade, i.e. a noun, which must take a capital letter.

 Toller Tipp!

If you want to generalise quantities and measures, you can use the following: *sehr* (very), *zu* (too), *viel* (a lot, much), *ganz* (all), *ziemlich* (quite), *ein wenig* (a little), *ein bisschen* (a bit):

> *Du bist sehr schön!*
> You are very pretty!

> *Ich habe viel Glück.*
> I have a lot of luck.

> *Du bist ganz nass.*
> You are all wet.

> *Ich bin ziemlich müde.*
> I'm quite tired.

> *Möchtest du ein wenig Wein?*
> Would you like a little wine?

> *Willst du ein bisschen Schokolade?*
> Do you want a bit of chocolate?

 **Fertig?**

1 Mehr oder weniger?

Richtig (R) oder falsch (F)? Verbessere die falschen Sätze!

True (R) or false (F)? Correct the wrong sentences!

1. Ein Liter Benzin kostet mehr als ein Kilo Kartoffeln.
2. Ein Glas Rotwein kostet mehr als ein Pfund Käse.
3. Tausend Gramm Butter wiegen mehr als ein Kilo Kohle.
4. Ein Fußballplatz ist im Durchschnitt 80 m lang mal 40 m breit.
5. Berlin ist sechshunderttausend Meter von Bonn entfernt.
6. Die Durchschnittstemperatur in einem Hallenbad ist 28 bis 30 Grad.
7. Mein Durchschnitt in Deutsch ist 4,5: das ist gut!
8. Mein Vater ist 1,60 groß und er wiegt 100 Kilo. Er ist ganz athletisch!
9. Ein Familienauto fährt normalerweise maximal 160 km/h.
10. Anderhalb Liter Olivenöl kosten weniger als ein Liter Wasser.

2 Ein Apfelkuchen – mein Lieblingsrezept!

Achtung! Deine Briefpartnerin ist zu Besuch. Sie bäckt einen guten Apfelkuchen, aber sie hat kein deutsches Rezept dabei. Du musst also die richtigen Mengen aus dem Kochbuch deiner Mutter übersetzen.

Attention! Your pen friend is visiting. She makes great German apple pie but has no recipe in German to hand. Using your mother's cookbook, you need to translate the quantities into clear German.

Die Zutaten:

... Weizenmehl   ... Backpulver
... Eier   ... Äpfel
... Milch   ... Zucker
... Butter bzw. Margarine

Anweisungen:

Tun Sie alle Zutaten in einen Mixer. Backen Sie den Kuchen ... Minuten lang in einem Elektroherd bei einer ... Temperatur von ... Celsius.

> *Mix the following ingredients together, using a food processor:*
>
> *3 eggs (medium)*   *100 ml milk*
> *120 g of butter/marg*   *170 g sugar*
> *10 g baking powder*   *1 lb cooking apples*
> *300 g plain flour*
>
> *Bake in a tin, in the centre of a hot electric oven: average temp. 190 ° C:*
> *1 hour 30 mins.*

3 Messen, wiegen, erstmals fragen?
Beantworte folgende Fragen! Schreibe volle Sätze mit Worten anstatt Ziffern!

Answer the following questions. Write complete sentences using words instead of numerals.

1. Wie groß bist du? (1,70 m)
2. Und deine Mutter? (1,65 m)
3. Was wiegst du? (73 kg)
4. Wie viel Wein gibt es in einer normalen Weinflasche? (0,7 l)
5. Wie viel Pfund sind anderthalb Kilo? (3,3 lb)
6. Welche Maße hat dieser Tisch?

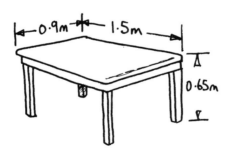

     Er ist... M l... , er ist ... Z ... b ..., er ist ... Z ... h ... .
7. Wie weit ist London von Bonn entfernt? (ca.550 km)
8. Welche Lufttemperatur haben wir im Sommer? (20–30 ° C)

Los!

4 Rate mal .... Was ist das? Wer ist das?
Schreibe 10 Erklärungen für Sachen oder Personen, die dein Partner bzw. deine Klasse später durch ihre Größe, ihr Gewicht oder ihre Entfernung identifizieren muss!

Write down 10 descriptions of people or things, by size, weight or distance, which your partner or class must then identify.

Beispiel:
1. Er ist ein Meter fünfzig groß.
2. Es liegt fünfhundert Meter vor dem Rathaus.
3. Sie ist achtzig Zentimeter breit.

5 Mein Lieblingsort
Beschreibe mit allen möglichen Maßen deinen Lieblingsort, z.B. ein Hotel aus dem Urlaub! Vergiss nicht, die Temperatur, die Entfernung in Kilometern, die Größe des Gebäudes zu erklären!

Use as many dimensions as possible to describe your favourite place, e.g. a hotel from your holidays. Don't forget to describe aspects like temperature, the distance in kilometres, the size of the building.

6 Meine Familie
Schreibe einen Brief an deinen deutschen Austauschpartner! Beschreibe dein Haus, wo du wohnst, wie weit das von der nächsten Stadt entfernt liegt, dein Schlafzimmer, deine Familie, was du trinkst und isst usw! Alle oben angegebenen Maße müssen mindestens einmal erwähnt werden: z.B. Zentimeter, Liter, Gramm, Meter.

Write a letter to your German exchange-partner. Describe your house, where you live, how far it is from the nearest town, your bedroom, your family, what you drink and eat, etc. All the measurements given above must be mentioned at least once, e.g. centimetres, litres, grammes, metres.

Glossar

die Kartoffeln	potatoes
die Kohle	coal
das Olivenöl	olive oil
messen	to measure
das Familienauto	family saloon car
entfernt	distant, away (from)
das Maß	measurement, dimension

10

WHO DOES WHAT?
nominative and accusative

 ## Auf die Plätze!

What does case mean?
The case tells us the **job or role** of a **noun** (Chapter 4) or **pronoun** (Chapter 22) within a sentence.

Endings added to many German words give helpful information: they tell the reader or listener whether a noun or pronoun is **masculine, feminine, neuter** or **plural**.

These **endings** also change to show us whether such words are the **subject** or **object** of the action. An incorrect ending does not always confuse the listener, but it can! When speaking, you have less time and less need to worry about this than **when writing**, when you do have the ability and the need to **check**.

■ **In German we already know one rule of position or word order:** the verb must always be the second idea. (See Chapter 1).

■ **It is the endings of the other words in a sentence and not their position, that tell us:**

– **who or what does** the action (**the subject**)
– who or what is the **target/victim/object** of that action (**the object**), thus:

Meine Schlange (**subject**) *beißt niemals meinen Bruder* (object).
means the same as:
Meinen Bruder (object) *beißt niemals meine Schlange* (**subject**).
My snake never bites my brother.

but NOT the same as:
Mein Bruder (**subject**) *beißt niemals meine Schlange* (object)!
My brother never bites my snake!

Pass auf!

In all these sentences the verb must be the second idea.

1 The nominative case

The nominative case describes the thing or person, who/which does the action (the **subject**):

*Mein Bruder heißt Robert. **Er** wohnt in Leipzig.*	masculine
*Wo arbeitet **deine Schwester**? Wie alt ist **sie**?*	feminine
*Wann startet **das Flugzeug**? **Es** ist verspätet!*	neuter
*Was sind **deine Eltern** von Beruf? Sind **sie** nett?*	plural

2 The accusative case

The accusative case, however, tells us that the person or thing is the **direct object** of the action:

*Ich habe ein**en** Bruder. Ich treffe **ihn** jeden Tag um vier Uhr.*	masculine
*Ich habe ein**e** Schwester! Wie findest du dein**e** Schwester?*	feminine
*Wir finden **das** Flugzeug praktisch. Wie findest du **es**?*	neuter
*Ich liebe mein**e** Eltern! Ich finde **sie** ganz nett!*	plural

 Toller Tipp!

Refer to the declension tables in Chapters 5 and 6 to remind you of the endings of *der, die, das* and *ein, eine, keinen* etc. (articles) and to Chapter 22 to check object pronouns (*ihn, ihm, sie, ihnen* etc.). Alternatively, a quick glance at Chapter 37 Appendix II might be enough.

 Pass auf!

Time expressions often require the **accusative**:
__Jeden Tag__ stehe ich um sieben Uhr auf.
__Diesen Monat__ haben wir keine Klassenarbeit!
*Kommst du **nächsten Freitag** in die Disko?*
__Nächstes Jahr__ fahren wir in die Schweiz.
*Wo wart ihr **letzten Sommer** auf Urlaub?*
__Diese Woche__ bin ich in Stuttgart.
*Wir waren **einen Monat lang** in Italien.*

 **Fertig?**

1 So ein Durcheinander!

Bring folgende Sätze in die richtige Reihenfolge!

Arrange the following sentences in the correct order.

1. Einen habe Großvater ich. Heißt er Thomas.
2. Lehrerin Mutter ist meine. Gern sie Salat isst.
3. Kaninchen du ein hast ? gut mein gefällt Kaninchen mir!
4. Zwei Eltern haben Autos meine. Autos alt sind beide etwas.
5. Brüder beißen Hund meinen niemals meine.
6. Diesen Klassenarbeit schreibt Brieffreund Montag eine mein.

2 Und noch mehr

Unterstreiche jetzt oben alle Subjekte (Nominativ) mit einem einfachem Strich und alle direkten Objekte (Akkusativ) mit einem Doppelstrich!

Now identify all the subjects (nominative) above with a single underline and all of the direct objects (accusative) with a double underline.

3 Lücken, Lücken überall

Fülle folgende Lücken mit den unten angegebenen Artikeln bzw. Pronomen aus!

Fill in the following gaps using articles or pronouns from the list below!

1. Entschuldigung! Wo liegt hier bitte … Dom (m)? Ist … weit von hier entfernt?
2. Also, … Dom finden Sie in der Stadtmitte. Nehmen sie … dritte Straße (f) links oder nehmen Sie … Bus (m), Linie Nr. 4.
3. Was ist …? Ist das … Hamster (m), … Maus (f) oder … Meerschweinchen (n)?
4. Ich weiß nicht, was … ist! Ich habe … Haustiere, aber ich möchte … Schlange (f)!
5. Wo ist … Heft (n)? Hast du … Heft vergessen?
6. Ja, … liegt zu Hause in meinem Schlafzimmer, aber … Bücher (pl) habe ich mit!
7. Wohin fahrt ihr … Jahr (n) auf Urlaub?
8. Also, … Sommer (m) fahren wir nach Spanien, aber …. Woche (f.) sind wir in Schottland.
9. … Eltern (pl.) wohnen in Berlin. … haben … Wohnung (f) am Stadtrand. Ich finde … ganz praktisch aber kalt!

sie	dein	keine	ein	den	dein	meine	er
meine	es	eine	sie	es	eine	das	ein
eine	der	die	den	nächstes	nächste	nächsten	

4 Noch mehr Lücken
Fülle folgende Lücken ohne Hilfe aus!

Fill in the following gaps without any help.

1. Wo ist m... Taschenrechner (m)? Hast du m... Taschenrechner gesehen?
2. Nein! Ist das d... Sporttasche (f)? Ich kann m... Sporttasche nicht finden!
3. Entschuldigung! Wo liegt hier bitte ... Verkehrsamt(n)? Ist ... weit von hier entfernt?
4. D... Verkehrsamt finden Sie vor dem Dom. ... ist ziemlich weit. Nehmen Sie d... Bus!
5. Welch... Kartoffeln (pl) esst ihr am liebsten?
6. Also, dies... holländischen Kartoffeln schmecken uns am besten.

Zur besseren Analyse könntest du in allen Sätzen den Nominativ einmal und den Akkusativ zweimal unterstreichen.

To show off your knowledge, you could underline the subject (nominative) in each sentence with a single line and the object (accusative) with a double line.

5 Bildertipps!
Jedes Bild (unten) passt zu einem Satz aus Übung 4. Schreibe für jedes Bild unten den passenden Satz!

Each of the pictures given below matches a sentence from Exercise 4. Write out the matching sentence for each picture.

Los!

6 *Was ich habe, was ich möchte!*

a. *Beschreibe dein Haus und deine Haustiere/deine Stadt/deine Einkäufe/deine Geburtstagswünsche.*

b. *Besser wird's, wenn das zu einem richtigen Dialog (mit Partner) wird:*

c. *Antworten auf diese Fragen sind eine Übung der Akkusativform.*

d. *Schreibe jetzt die Antworten auf solche Fragen auf.*
   – vielleicht sogar mit Unterstreichung der Objekte wie in früheren Übungen dieses Kapitels.

a. Describe your house, your pets, your town, what you would like when shopping or for your birthday.

b. Better still, create a dialogue with a partner. Ask and answer questions.

c. You have been automatically practising the accusative case by answering these questions.

d. Now, write your answers to all of these questions. Why don't you underline the objects as in previous exercises in this chapter?

Beispiel:

A. Hast du Geschwister/Haustiere?
   Was möchtest du zum Geburtstag?
   Was gibt es in deinem Schlafzimmer?
   Was kaufst du gern?

GLOSSAR

das Kaninchen	rabbit
weit ... entfernt	far away
das Meerschweinchen	guinea pig
der Taschenrechner	pocket calculator
die Kartoffel	potato
schmecken	to taste
beide	both
auf Urlaub	on holiday
praktisch	handy, useful
das Verkehrsamt	tourist information office
so ein Mist!	what a mess!

11

WITHOUT A PROBLEM
accusative with prepositions

 ## Auf die Plätze!

What are prepositions?
These words are always placed, or **POSITIONED**, before **(PRE-)** <u>the noun</u> which they affect:

> *Um <u>Mitternacht</u> fahren Autos **ohne** <u>Problem</u> **durch** <u>den Tunnel</u>.*
> **At** <u>midnight</u>, cars drive **through** <u>the tunnel</u> **without** any <u>problem</u>.

Hence the name: **PRE-POSITION!**

The accusative case is applied to the direct object, but also affects nouns, pronouns or articles when they follow certain **prepositions**, thus:

bis[†]	until, as far as	*durch*	through, by means of
für	for	*gegen*	against (physically), towards,
ohne	without		about (time-wise)
wider	in opposition to,	*um*	around (a place), at (a time)
	against (mentally)	*entlang*[‡]	along

 ### Pass auf!

1. **entlang**[‡] is **post-positioned**, **after** <u>the noun which it affects</u>:

   *Sie suchen den Dom? Also, fahren Sie <u>diese Straße</u> **entlang bis zur*** Ampel …*

2. **bis**[†] is quite often followed by *zu**, which takes the dative (see Chapter 12).

Toller Tipp!

If you exclude **entlang** and **bis** as exceptions (but do not forget them – they are important), the first letters of these prepositions can be learnt using the mnemonic:

 # Fertig?

1 P-zon-loch! (Präposition-loch)
Mit Hilfe der oben angegebenen Präpositionen füll folgende Lücken aus!

Use the prepositions given above to fill in the following gaps!

1. Ich fahre niemals auf Urlaub … meinen Fotoapparat.
2. … meinen Willen muss ich um sechs Uhr aufstehen!
3. In der Bundesliga hat München 2:0 … Dortmund gewonnen.
4. Wir haben eine Rundfahrt … die Altstadt gemacht.
5. Nächstes Jahr fahren wir … den Kanaltunnel nach Frankreich.
6. Jeden Samstag gehe ich … meine Oma einkaufen.
7. Letztes Jahr sind wir den Rhein … in die Schweiz heruntergefahren.

2 In Ordnung!
Ordne folgende Sätze! Vergiss nicht: Zeit vor Ort! (Siehe Kapitel 23)

Put the words in the following sentences into the correct order. Remember: time, manner, place! (See Chapter 23.)

1. Hausaufgaben   Mutti   !   machen   mich   kannst   du   für   meine   ?
2. Ein   Motorrad   Willen   meines   Vaters   ich   wider   möchte   .
3. Satellit   kann   ich   deutsche   Fernsehprogramme   durch   bekommen   .
4. Heute   Abend   in   die   gehen   um   Disko   zwanzig   Uhr   wir   .
5. Nach   Berlin   entlang   fahren   am   besten   Autobahn   die   Sie   !
6. Deinen   Tee   ohne   mit   Milch   oder   nimmst   du   ?
7. Verloren   unsere   Partnerschule   null   zu   vier   wir   haben   gegen   !
8. Nächsten   Tschüs   !   Samstag   bis   !

3 Stau um Hamburg
Fülle folgende Lücken ohne Hilfe aus!

Fill in the following gaps without help.

Von Hannover … Kiel sind's etwa zweihundert Kilometer. Wir fahren immer die Autobahn …, … den Elbtunnel, … die Großstadt Hamburg herum und … Pause! Es gibt nämlich jeden Tag … vier Uhr abends immer Probleme mit den Autos. Letztes Jahr haben wir … meinen Willen eine Kaffeepause … meine Oma gemacht und von siebzehn … achtzehn Uhr sind wir im Elbtunnel stehen geblieben. Schrecklich!

4 Bilder sprechen Bände!
Schreibe die Sätze auf, die zu den folgenden Bildern passen.

From Exercises 1 to 3 certain sentences are represented in the following pictures. Write down the sentences which match.

 # Los!

5 Probleme, Probleme!

Schreibe einen Brief bzw. eine Postkarte an deinen Brieffreund! Beschreibe eine Reise, wo du Probleme hattest! Nimm Beispiele und Präpositionen aus diesem Kapitel als Modell!

Write a letter or postcard to your pen friend. Describe a journey in which you too had problems. Take examples and prepositions from this chapter as a model.

6 Um die Stadt ... ohne Probleme!

Für jede Präposition oben schreibe möglichst viele Ausdrücke, die du kennst! Vergleich deine Liste mit deinem Partner! Wer hat die meisten?

For each of the above prepositions list as many expressions as you know. Compare your list with your partner's. Who has most?

Beispiel:

bis	**bis** Samstag!
	bis bald!
	bis nächste Woche!
	bis ...

Glossar

stehen bleiben	to get stuck, stop still
Verkehrsprobleme	traffic problems
der Wille (-n)	will, wish(es)
die Bundesliga	football league
der Kanaltunnel	Channel Tunnel
verloren	lost
Tschüs!	bye!
auf Urlaub	on holiday
der Fotoapparat	camera
aufstehen	to get up
die Rundfahrt	tour
das Motorrad	motorbike
gewonnen	won

12

WHO DOES WHAT TO WHOM?
dative with prepositions

 **Auf die Plätze!**

Recognising the dative

In Chapter 10 you will see how German uses **endings** to distinguish between the **subject** (nominative) and the **direct object** (accusative), whilst in English the order of the words tells us what their roles are. Now apply this rule to the following:

A As a birthday present, I gave my sister my snake.

B Now change the word order for sister and snake!

In German, the difference between the direct object and the indirect object is shown in the **endings**, so that there is no confusion!

		subject	indirect object	direct object
A	*Zum Geburtstag gab* (gave snake to sister)	*ich*	*meiner Schwester*	*meine Schlange.*
B	*Zum Geburtstag gab* (gave sister to snake)	*ich*	*meiner Schlange*	*meine Schwester!*

We see or hear the difference of the **indirect object** (mein**er** Schwester/mein**er** Schlange) in its **dative ending**.

Of course, English can make this difference clearer by using the preposition 'to':

	subject	direct object	indirect object
As a birthday present	I	gave a snake	*to* my sister.

Prepositions and the dative

German also uses the **dative** after a certain number of **prepositions**:

aus	out of, originating from, made of	*seit*	since/for
bei	at the (house/shop) of…,		(period of past time)
	in the event of…	*von*	of, from, by
mit	with, by (transport)	*zu*	to, at
nach	after, to(wards)	*außer*	except for/ out of (order)
		*gegenüber	opposite

 Pass auf!

> **Gegenüber*, like *entlang*, can be **post-positioned**,
> i.e. placed **after** the object to which it refers:
>
> *Ich wohne **gegenüber** dem Bahnhof.*
> or: *Ich wohne dem Bahnhof **gegenüber**.*

■ The prepositions *zu, von, bei* often combine with the article to form a compound:

*zu + dem = **zum***	*zu + der = **zur***
*bei + dem = **beim***	*von + dem = **vom***

■ *zu* is commonly used for important occasions:

zum *Geburtstag*   **zu** *Weihnachten*   **zu** *Ostern*

■ Certain common verbs and verbal phrases automatically attract the dative:

helfen	z.B.	*Kannst du **mir** helfen?*
gefallen	z.B.	*Das Hotel hat **uns** gut gefallen.*
schmecken	z.B.	*Hoffentlich schmeckt es **Ihnen**.*
Gesundheit	z.B.	***Mir** ist schlecht.*
		*Wann hast du **dir** das*
		Bein gebrochen?
Temperatur	z.B.	***Mir** ist warm/ist **euch** zu kalt?*

■ Certain, often common, nouns take an ending in the dative cases:

*Ich muss (mit) Herr**n** Fischer sprechen.*   (i.e. **to** Mr. Fischer)

– this is why we address a letter **to** Mr. Fischer as *Herr**n** Fischer.*

*Auf Arbeitspraktikum musste ich ein**em** Kund**en** helfen*   (*helfen* + **dative**)

(See weak nouns, Chapter 4)

Fertig ?

1 Was fehlt?
Fülle folgende Lücken mit Hilfe der oben angegebenen Präpositionen aus!

Fill in the following gaps using the prepositions given above.

1. … dir kommen zehn andere Gäste … meiner Geburtstagsfeier.
2. Woher kommst du? Ich komme … Großbritannien.
3. … welchem Gleis fährt der nächste Zug nach Nürnberg?
4. Ich lerne … drei Jahren Deutsch.
5. Ich wohne … fünf Jahren der Bäckerei ….
6. Wenn es regnet, fahre ich … der Straßenbahn zur Schule.
7. … Weihnachten habe ich … meinen Eltern eine Stereoanlage bekommen.
8. … schlechtem Wetter ist der Skilift immer … Betrieb!
9. In den Osterferien habe ich … meinem Onkel und meiner Tante gewohnt.
10. Kommst du heute Abend … uns? Wir wohnen deinem Partner direkt …!

2 Dativ – mit oder ohne Präposition?
Fülle folgende Lücken mit Hilfe der unten angegebenen Präpositionen oder Pronomen aus!

Fill in the following gaps using the prepositions or pronouns given in the list below.

1. Von … Vater habe ich … letzten Geburtstag eine Uhr … Holz bekommen.
2. Kommst du heute Abend mit …… Eissporthalle?
3. … gutem Wetter gehe ich immer zu Fuß zur Arbeit.
4. Was machst du nach … Mittagspause?
5. Kann ich … bei deinen Hausaufgaben helfen?
6. Seit … Jahr wohnt mein bester Freund … Bahnhof gegenüber.

zum	dir	aus	zur	einem	bei	meinem	dem	der	mir

3 Dativ: jetzt bis du daran!

Fülle die Lücken ohne Hilfe aus! Siehe auch die Tabelle von Artikeln in den Kapiteln 5, 6, 22, 37!

Fill in the gaps without help. Refer also to the tables of articles in Chapters 5, 6, 22 or 37.

1. Seit ein… Jahr (n.) wohnen wir d… Bibliothek (f.) direkt gegenüber.
2. Bei dies… schönen Wetter (n.) fahre ich mit d… Fahrrad (n.) in die Schule.
3. Nach d… Morgenpause (f.) habe ich Kunst bei Herr… Thomas.
4. Kannst du m… helfen? Außer d… habe ich keine guten Freunde!
5. Die Lautsprecher von mein… Stereoanlage (f.) sind aus schwarzen Holz (n.).
6. Nächstes Jahr fahre ich mit mein… Eltern (pl.) mit d… Auto (n.) in d… Schweiz (f.).

Los!

4 Gib's ihm, gib's ihr, zeig's mir!

A. Übe erstmals (mit einem Partner) Akkusativformen durch die Ausdrücke:

> *Gib mir … (z.B.) … einen Radiergummi/eine Armbanduhr/ein Heft.*
>
> *oder: Zeig mir… (z.B.) … deinen besten Freund/deine Hausaufgaben usw.*

B. Übe dann in einer gemischten Gruppe die dritte Person im Dativ durch die Ausdrücke:

Gib deinem Partner	*einen Radiergummi, deine Armbanduhr, dein Heft…*
bzw. Zeig deiner Partnerin	*einen Radiergummi, deine Armbanduhr, dein Heft…*
oder sogar Gib deinen Partnern	*ein Buch, deine Adresse, die Hand usw.*

Wer kann die meisten Befehle geben?

A. Practise the accusative form of objects (with a partner), using the expressions shown above.
B. Then practise speaking to others in a mixed group, using the third person dative in the expressions highlighted above.

Who can give most commands?

5 Wie kommt man am besten dahin?

A. Sprich mit einem Partner und schreibt alle Transportmittel auf!

Beispiele:

mit dem Bus (m.)	**zu** Fuß
mit der U-Bahn (f.)	**zu** Pferd
mit dem Auto (n.)	usw.

B. Dann übt mit einer unterschiedlichen Farbe Reiseziele.

Beispiele:

zum Bahnhof	**nach** Deutschland
zur Schule	**in die** Schweiz
zum Stadtzentrum	**in die** Vereinigten Staaten

*C. Schreibe jetzt volle Sätze, wo alle Transportmittel und Reiseziele erwähnt **werden**!*

Beispiele:

Man fährt **mit der** U-Bahn **in den** Vereinigten Staaten!
Fährst du heute **mit der** U-Bahn **zur** Stadtmitte?

Vergiss nicht: Zeit vor Ort (Kapitel 23).
Be careful! Don't forget: time, manner, place (Chapter 23).

A. Practise aloud and then write up (with a partner) as many means of transport as you can think of.
B. Then, in a different colour, practice as many destinations as possible.
C. Now write out complete sentences, including all the modes of transport and destinations.
   (See the examples given above).

6 Geflügelte Worte

Einmal geübt, lassen sich oben erwähnte Redewendungen eventuell im Klassenzimmer, bzw. im Studierzimmer zur Erinnerung an die Dativformen aufhängen. Viel Spaß!

Once practised, these expressions can be designed, perhaps on a computer, as a logo, and even in a preferred colour, to be hung up on the wall in your classroom or study as reminders of the dative.
Have fun!

Beispiel:

GLOSSAR

der Kunde	customer (weak noun)
die Geburtstagsfeier	birthday celebration
der Lautsprecher	loudspeaker
Weihnachten	Christmas
das Gleis	platform, line
die Gesundheit	health
der Gast	guest
das Holz	wood
in Betrieb	in working order
außer Betrieb	out of order

13

TO OR AT THE BEACH
accusative/dative with prepositions

 **Auf die Plätze!**

Accusative for motion, dative for position!
German clearly distinguishes between the **accusative** case (for **direct** objects) and the **dative** (for **indirect** objects).

The **accusative** must also be used after one **group of prepositions** and the **dative** after another: see Chapters 11 and 12.

The **largest** and **perhaps most common group of prepositions** requires our particular attention:

an	at (the side of), on	*über*	over, about, via
auf	on (top of)	*unter*	under, among
hinter	behind	*vor*	before, in front of, *ago
in	in(to), in(side)	*zwischen*	between
neben	next to		

■ This group of prepositions attracts the **accusative** when indicating **motion**:

  'in**to**', 'on**to**' in English

  BUT the **dative** when referring to static **position**:

  'in'(**side**), 'on' (**top of**)

■ The **accusative** is also generally used to suggest **a mental 'thrust' of activity**:
  talking **about**
  thinking **about**
  casting your mind back **to** (i.e. remembering …)

■ The **accusative** is used when **putting** things **in**(to), **on**(to), or **under** another object, since **motion** is involved after verbs like *stellen*, *legen*, *setzen* and *stecken*.

■ *an ... vorbei* (= (going) past/by...), attracts the dative case:
Unterwegs zum Bahnhof fahren wir **am** *Kino* **vorbei**.

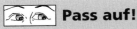 **Pass auf!**

1 Most of the above prepositions, when followed by *das* or *dem* can **contract**, thus:

Accusative	**Dative**
an + das = ***ans***	*an + dem =* ***am***
auf + das = ***aufs***	*hinter + dem =* ***hinterm***
in + das = ***ins***	*in + dem =* ***im***
über + das = ***übers***	*über + dem =* ***überm***

2 **vor*** (= ago) is placed, as a **pre**position, **before** the noun referred to:

Vor zwei Wochen   two weeks **ago**

 # Fertig?

1 Mischmasch

Bring folgende Sätze in die richtige Reihenfolge!

Put the following sentences together in the correct order.

1. Verkehrsamt komme zum besten am ich wie ?
2. Dem Theater hinter auf liegt der rechten Seite die Realschule .
3. Wand ich eine Kuckucksuhr habe meinem in an der Zimmer .
4. Diese Messer auf den Tisch lege ich oder in die Schublade kommen sie ?
5. Geradeaus Kreuzung fahren Sie bis hier zur .
6. Dem Eiscafé das Kino und der Post finden Sie zwischen .
7. Wohnte ich hinterm vor zwei Jahren der und neben Schloss Stadthalle .
8. Erzählen über Lieblingsthema etwas mein ich möchte .

2 P-zon-loch!

Fülle die Lücken mit den unten angegebenen Präpositionen bzw. Artikeln aus!

Use the prepositions or articles in the box below to fill in the following gaps.

1. Was steht hier … der Speisekarte (f.)? Wie heißt das … Englisch?
2. Jeden Morgen liegen meine Bücher auf … Tisch (m.). Ich lege sie schnell in … Tasche (f.).
3. Treffen wir uns nach … Mittagessen (n.) vor … Sportplatz (m.)! Alles klar?
4. Wollen wir lieber … Kino (n.) gehen? Was läuft eigentlich … Kino?
5. In … Winterferien (pl.) sind wir in … Alpen (pl.) gefahren.
6. … Wochenende (n.) fahre ich gern an … Strand (m.) und ich sonne mich … der See (f.).
7. 'Spiegel, Spiegel an … Wand (f.): wer ist die Schönste … ganzen Land (n.)?'
8. Gehen wir in … Kaufhalle (f.)! Dort sind alle CDs (pl.) … Sonderangebot!
9. Wir fahren gern Sonntags auf … Land (n.), ich möchte eines Tages auf … Lande wohnen!
10. 'Gibt es eine Telefonzelle hier in … Nähe (f.)?'
    'Ja, … dem Dom (m.) und … Bushaltestelle**n** (pl.), da drüben!'

am	im	dem	auf	meine	dem	ins	den	die	dem	auf
zwischen	dem	im	den	der	im	das	der	den	die	an

Los!

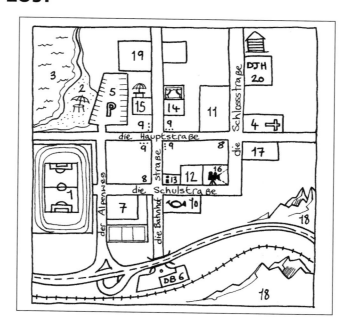

Key to map:

1. der Sportplatz
2. der Strand
3. der See
4. der Dom
5. der Parkplatz
6. der Bahnhof

7. die Realschule
8. die Kreuzung
9. die Ampel
10. die Post
11. die Stadthalle
12. die Kaufhalle

13. das Verkehrsamt
14. das Theater
15. das Eiscafé
16. das Kino
17. das Schloss
18. die Alpen
19. das Hotel Seeblick
20. die Jugendherberge

3 Wegweiser!

Du (A) stehst vor dem Verkehrsamt (13) in Alpendorf! Frag einen Partner (B), wie du von hier aus zu drei verschiedenen Orten kommst! Dein Partner versucht, möglichst viele Präpositionen anzuwenden. Wechselt dann die Rollen!

You (A) are outside the tourist information centre (13) in Alpendorf. Ask your partner (B) how to get to three different places. Your partner should try to use as many prepositions in the answer as possible. Now change roles!

Beispiel:

A Wie komme ich am besten *zum Dom?*

B Gehen Sie hier *die Bahnhofstraße entlang. An der Ampel* gehen Sie rechts bis *zur Kreuzung.* Der Dom liegt *gegenüber dem Schloss.*

4 Ein Brief: ein Treffpunkt

Schreibe einen Brief an deinen Brieffreund, der dich in Alpendorf besuchen will! Beschreibe deinen Wohnort in Alpendorf und den Weg vom Bahnhof! Verwende möglichst viele Präpositionen! Dein Partner muss auf einer Kopie des Stadtplans den richtigen Weg mit Farbe einzeichnen.

Write a letter to your pen pal who wants to visit you in Alpendorf. Describe where you live in Alpendorf and the route from the station. Use as many prepositions as possible. On a copy of the map your partner must then trace the correct route using a coloured pen.

Transferübung!

Das gleiche kann man mit einem Plan eines Hauses, des Schulgeländes, eines Hotels, einer Autobahnraststätte, eines Flughafens, einer Küche, eines Schlafzimmers, usw. machen.

Once practised, such exercises can be transposed to another context, e.g. the layout of a house, the school, a hotel, a motorway service area, an airport, a kitchen, a bedroom, etc.

GLOSSAR

stellen	to position (upright)
setzen	to place (covering)
legen	to lay, place (horizontally)
stecken	to 'stick' sth. inside
erzählen	to tell/give an account
das Verkehrsamt	tourist information centre
eine Kuckucksuhr	cuckoo clock
die Realschule	technical high school
das Lieblingsthema	favourite topic
geradeaus	straight on
die Ampel	traffic lights
die Kreuzung	crossroads
die Bushaltestelle	bus stop
die Stadthalle	festival hall
die Kaufhalle	shopping store
die Schublade	drawer
die Speisekarte	menu

14

INSTEAD OF WORK
genitive with prepositions

 Auf die Plätze!

What is the genitive?
The genitive describes the possession or connection '**of**' someone or something to another:

Die Farbe meines Fahrrads ist rot.   The colour **of** my bike is red.
Die Mutter meiner Freundin   My girlfriend**'s** mother is a
ist Firmenleiterin.   company manager.

Certain German prepositions naturally take the genitive:

(an) statt	instead of…	*infolge…*	as a result of…
innerhalb	inside (of)…, within	*während*	during
außerhalb	outside (of)…, excluding	*wegen*	because of
diesseits	on this side of	*beiderseits*	on both sides of…
jenseits	on that side of/beyond…	*trotz*	in spite of…

 Pass auf!

In English we often use **…'s** to show the **genitive**. German can do this too, but normally uses **no apostrophe**:

Das Auto meines Vaters ist grün.   My father**'s** car is green.
Meines Vaters Auto ist grün.

German often avoids the genitive by using the preposition *von* **+ dative**:

Das Auto von meinem Vater ist grün.   My father**'s** car is green.

Grammatik Aktiv!

 **Fertig?**

1 So ein Mist!
Dein Briefpartner hat dir einen Brief mit dem Computer geschrieben, aber der Drucker hat ein Problem und alle Präpositionen sind durcheinander geraten! Setz die treffenden Präpositionen in die richtigen Lücken!

Your pen friend has word-processed a letter to you but the printer has a problem with prepositions! You will find them in a jumble at the bottom. Put the appropriate prepositions in the correct gaps.

Potsdam, den 2. Februar.

Liebe(r) Chris,

... meiner Klassenarbeiten musste ich ... der letzten paar Wochen so viel lernen, dass ich keine Zeit zum Briefschreiben hatte. Entschuldigung!

... meiner heutigen Hausaufgaben schreibe ich dir doch endlich einige Worte. Siehst du meine neue Adresse? Ja! ... der neuen Arbeitsstelle meines Vaters sind wir nach Potsdam umgezogen. Das ist eine schöne alte Stadt ... von Berlin. Vor vielen Jahren konnten meine westdeutschen Eltern Potsdam kaum besuchen. Diese kulturreiche historische Stadt lag damals ... der Ost-West-Grenze Deutschlands in der ehemaligen DDR.

Wir haben jetzt eine hübsche alte Villa in direkter Nähe des historischen Schlosses „Sanssouci".

... der Stadt haben wir Wälder und Parkgelände. Auf der anderen Seite liegt ein schöner breiter See. Ich schicke dir einen kleinen Plan von der Villa, siehst du? ... des Hauses haben wir eine richtige Küche –... der kleinen Kochecke von unserer alten Wohnung in Köln! ... der Terrasse gibt's sogar ein kleines Freibad: ideal zum Eistanzen im Winter!

Bis bald,
dein(e) Ulli

---

innerhalb	infolge	während	anstatt	jenseits
wegen	trotz	außerhalb	jenseits	diesseits

90

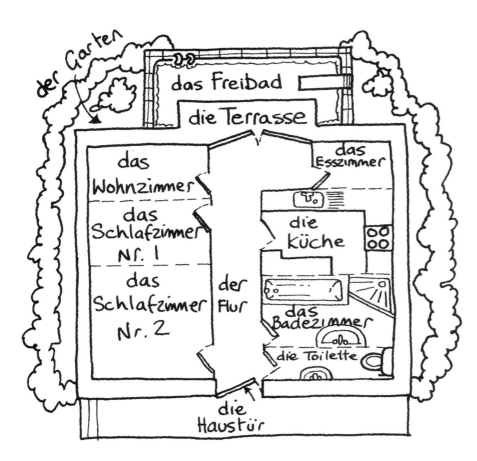

2 P-zon-loch!

Fülle folgende Lücken mit Hilfe der unten angegebenen Artikel bzw. Possessiven aus!

Fill in the following gaps, using the articles or possessives from the box below.

1. Diesseits … Grenze (f.) ist Deutschland und jenseits ist Polen.
2. Außerhalb … Hausaufgaben (pl.) muss ich Klavier üben!
3. Während … Sommerferien (pl.) sind wir in die Türkei geflogen.
4. Trotz … Vaters möchte ich ein Motorrad fahren!
5. Wegen … kleineren Geschwister (pl.) muss ich heute Abend zu Hause bleiben.
6. Ich hätte lieber ein T-Shirt anstatt … Hemdes (n.).
7. Während … Arbeitspraktikums (n.) durften wir innerhalb … Arbeitsstunden (pl.) nicht rauchen!
8. Infolge … schlechten Wetters (n.) konnte ich letzte Woche nicht ausgehen. Innerhalb … ganzen Woche (f.) habe ich nur Hausaufgaben geschrieben, Romane gelesen und ferngesehen: wie langweilig!

unseres	der	unserer	meiner	des	der	meines	eines	der	meiner

Los!

3 Alles zusammen!

Du hast auch ein neues Haus und schreibst an Ulli zurück. Beschreibe dein Haus mit möglichst vielen Präpositionen aus den letzten Kapiteln (11–14) – vor allem mit dem Genitiv! Der Plan von Ullis Haus könnte dir helfen.

You too have just moved to a new house. Write back to Ulli, describing it with as many prepositions from Chapters 11–14 as possible. Try to use the genitive in particular. Ulli's lay-out of his house might help you.

4 Partnerarbeit: besser zu zweit!

A   Kopier (vielleicht mit einem Partner) eine interessante Broschüre von (einem Hotel aus) einer deutschsprachigen Stadt! Leg einen Plan dabei!

B   Mit 'Tintenkiller' oder mit gepunkteten Lücken lösch alle Präpositionen, so dass ein Lückentext entsteht!

C   Gib deinen Lückentext an andere aus deiner Klasse weiter! Können sie ihn richtig ausfüllen?

A   (Maybe with a partner) copy an interesting brochure about (a hotel in) a German-speaking town. Add a relevant map of the town. You could word-process your own copy.

B   Now use ink-eraser to remove all the prepositions until you have a gapped text.

C   Give copies to others in the class. Can they fill it in correctly?

5 Schule muss nicht langweilig sein!

A   Schreib(vielleicht zu zweit) einen Bericht über deine Schule, das Schulgelände, den Stundenplan, das Schuljahr – alles außer der Schuluniform!

B   Versuch dabei möglichst viele verschiedene Präpositionen einzubauen und vielleicht den Akkusativ, Dativ und Genitiv mit einer Farbe zu identifizieren!

C   Versuch allein einen Bericht über deine letzten Ferien oder dein Arbeitspraktikum zu schreiben! Ein Plan, eine Postkarte, eine Landkarte könnte dabei helfen!

A   Write a report about your school, the grounds, the timetable, the school year, etc. but not school uniform! You could write with a partner.

B   Try to build in as many prepositions as possible. You might then like to highlight those prepositions that take each different case – accusative, dative, genitive, with a particular colour-code.

C   Try, similarly, to write an *individual* account of your last holiday or your work experience. A plan, postcard or map might help.

GLOSSAR

die Grenze	border, frontier
das Arbeitspraktikum	work experience
die Arbeitsstunden	working hours
die Arbeitsstelle	post, job
die ehemalige DDR	former East Germany
das Eistanzen	figure skating
die Kochecke	kitchen area
umgezogen	moved
kaum	hardly
hübsch	pretty
der Wald	forest
das Gelände	grounds
ein Roman	novel
doch	however

15

I LIVE, SHE IS, THEY HAVE
present tense

 ## Auf die Plätze!

What is a verb?
A **verb** is a word representing:

    A. an **action**   →   I **play** …, you **make** …
    B. a **state**   →   we **have**, they **are**, I am **becoming**

What is the present tense?
The **present tense** is the form which we give the verb to show that it:

■ **happens regularly, for example:**

    *Ich **lese** jeden Tag*   I **read** every day
    *Was **lernst** du in der Schule?*   What **do** you **learn** at school? (regularly)

  or,

■ **is happening now, for example:**

    *Ruhe! Ich **lese**!*   Quiet! I **am reading**! (i.e. at the moment)
    *Was **lernst** du in Informatik?*   What **are** you **learning** in I.T.?

 **Pass auf!**

    German uses one word for the verb in the present tense:
        lese   =   I read/I am reading
                Simple!

    Ignore the trimmings which we often put around the verb in English:

        am read**ing**/**do** you … read …?

1 Infinitive, stem, endings

German has four major groups of verbs:

a	**weak or regular** = they follow the rules	(see Chapter 15)
b	**irregular** = a law unto themselves!	(see Chapter 15)
c	**strong** = only partially headstrong …!	(see Chapter 16)
d	**modal** = these **can** and **should** be easily learnt!	(see Chapter 17)

It is easiest if we compare the shape of some common examples:

a Weak verbs

	Infinitive	*wohnen* (**to** live)	*spielen* (**to** play)	*machen* (**to** do)
	Subject pronoun			
SINGULAR	*ich*	*wohne*	*spiele*	*mache*
	du	*wohnst*	*spielst*	*machst*
	er, sie, es, man	*wohnt*	*spielt*	*macht*
PLURAL	*wir*	*wohnen*	*spielen*	*machen*
	Sie (formal/ also sing.)	*wohnen*	*spielen*	*machen*
	ihr	*wohnt*	*spielt*	*macht*
	sie	*wohnen*	*spielen*	*machen*

The **endings** of one regular verb:

■ are exactly the same as for the other verbs: (*-e, -est, -t, -en, -t*)

■ change only according to the **subject** (the person who **does** the action):

   du…, wir…, sie …etc.

■ are added to the **stem** of the verb.

   The stem of regular verbs is simply the **infinitive** form **minus the *-en*.**

   e.g. ***wohn-, spiel-, mach-***

Grammatik Aktiv!

Subject pronouns (see also Ch. 22,37).

SINGULAR	1. I	*ich*	-e
	2. you (singular,friendly)	*du*	-(e)st
	3. he, she, it, one (generally)	*er, sie, es, man*	-t
PLURAL	1. we	*wir*	
	2. you (formal/also singular)	*Sie*	} -en
	3. they	*sie*	
	4. you (plural,friendly)	*ihr*	-(e)t

 Pass auf!

sie (she), *Sie* (you: formal) and *sie* (they) will not be confused as long as you :

A. check their **spelling**, for the capital or small case letter.
B. check their **verb ending**!

 Toller Tipp!

Er, *sie* (she), *es* and *man* all refer to the same idea, a 'third person, singular', and always share the same verb ending: *-t*.

Wir, *Sie* (you) and *sie* (they) forms, in the plural, also share the same ending: *-en*.

b Irregular verbs

Now apply your knowledge to our second group, **irregular verbs**:

Infinitive	*hab*en (to have)	*sei*n (to be)	*werd*en (to become)
Subject pronoun			
SINGULAR *ich*	*habe*	*bin*	*werde*
du	*hast*	*bist*	*wirst*
er, sie, es	*hat*	*ist*	*wird*
PLURAL *wir* *Sie* (formal, also singular) *sie*	*haben*	*sind*	*werden*
ihr	*habt*	*seid*	*werdet*

Learn these three verbs thoroughly, preferably aloud, using the above tips.
They are the most common and important verbs in German!
You will need them **to form other tenses**.

 ## Fertig?

1 Verben und Lücken
Fülle folgende Lücken (mit Hilfe des Infinitivs) aus!

Fill in the following gaps (with the help of the infinitive).

Regelmäßige Verben   Regular verbs

1. Wie … du? (heißen)
2. Ich … in Großbritannien. (wohnen)
3. Wann … wir Basketball? (spielen)
4. Was … ihr heute Abend? (machen)
5. Entschuldigen Sie. Wann … man hier zu*? (*zumachen).
6. Wir … Deutsch seit drei Jahren. (studieren)
7. Das ist meine Brieffreundin. Sie … in Zürich. (wohnen)
8. In England … es sehr oft im Winter. (regnen)
9. Sind Sie Herr Wittkowski? … Sie schon lange auf uns? (warten)
10. Wie oft … du Karten? (spielen)

2 Andere Verben, andere Lücken!
Fülle folgende Lücken (mit Hilfe des Infinitivs) aus!

Fill in the following gaps (with the help of the infinitive).

Unregelmäßige Verben   Irregular verbs

1. Ich … fünfzehn Jahre alt. (sein)
2. … du Geschwister? (haben)
3. Mit wie vielen Jahren … man normalerweise Student? (werden)
4. Toll! Heute … wir keine Hausaufgaben! (haben)
5. Entschuldigung, … Sie Frau Wittkowski? (sein)
6. Mein Austauschpartner … sechzehn. Er … in der 10. Klasse. (sein)
7. Was für Schulfächer … ihr heute? (haben)
8. Nächste Woche … meine Schwester Geburtstag. (haben)
9. Sie … achtzehn Jahre alt. (werden)
10. Das Wetter ist jetzt schöner: es … endlich sonnig! (werden)

3 Welches Verb? Welche Form?

Verbinde die linke Seite (1–10) mit der rechten Seite (A–J)!

Match up the left side (1–10) with the right (A–J).

1. Meine Eltern wohnen nicht zusammen.
2. Lernen Sie schon lange Englisch?
3. Dieses Jahr werde ich vierzehn.
4. Das Sommerwetter ist hier sehr sonnig!
5. Seid ihr Österreicher?
6. Wir haben Ende Februar Winterferien.
7. Spielst du ein Instrument?
8. Wo wohnt deine Schwester?
9. Wann werdet ihr fertig?
10. Was machen Sie am Wochenende?

A. Ja, sind die Tage immer so warm?
B. Sie sind ideal zum Skifahren.
C. Sind sie geschieden?
D. Wie lange lernen Sie es?
E. Wir haben keine festen Pläne.
F. Sie hat eine Wohnung in der Stadtmitte.
G. Wir machen Hausaufgaben bis neun Uhr.
H. Ja? Wann hast du Geburtstag?
I. Ja, ich lerne seit drei Jahren Klavier.
J. Nein, wir sind aus Liechtenstein.

Los!

4 Ein erster Brief

Schreibe einen ersten Brief an deinen neuen Briefpartner! Erkläre, wer du bist und wo du wohnst! Beschreibe deine Familie, ihre Beschäftigung und einen typischen Tag am Wochenende bzw. in der Schule!

Write your first letter to your new pen friend. Explain who you are and where you live. Describe your family and what they do. Describe a typical day at the weekend or, alternatively, at school.

5 Geflügelte Worte!

Zeichne ein Poster für dein Klassenzimmer, dein Arbeitszimmer, dein Büro! Erkläre mit einem Satz, mit einem Verb, was man im Bild macht, z.B. 'Hier lernt man Deutsch!' Du könntest das eventuell im Studierzimmer bzw. Klassenzimmer aufhängen.

Design a poster for your classroom, your own study, your office. With one verb, in one sentence, explain the activity shown in your visual , e.g. 'Hier lernt man Deutsch!' You might like to hang it up in your study or classroom.

GLOSSAR

geschieden	divorced
Schulfächer (pl.)	school subjects
regnen	to rain
warten auf	to wait for
zumachen	to close/'shut *up* shop'.
dunkel	dark
feste Pläne	set/pre-arranged plans
fertig (*werden*)	to finish

16

I SPEAK, YOU READ, WE WEAR
the present tense of strong verbs

 **Auf die Plätze!**

In Chapter 15, two of the four groups of verbs are introduced. These are:

- **regular (weak)**, and

- **irregular**.

Now study the following tables of the third group, known as **strong verbs**: identify a pattern.

Infinitive		*tragen*	*fahren*	*sprechen*	*essen*	*lesen*	*sehen*
	to…	carry/ wear	travel/ go	speak	eat	read	see
Subject							
	ich	*trage*	*fahre*	*spreche*	*esse*	*lese*	*sehe*
	du	*trägst*	*fährst*	*sprichst*	*isst*	*liest*	*siehst*
	er, sie, es, man	*trägt*	*fährt*	*spricht*	*isst*	*liest*	*sieht*
	wir *Sie* *sie*	*tragen*	*fahren*	*sprechen*	*essen*	*lesen*	*sehen*
	ihr	*tragt*	*fahrt*	*sprecht*	*esst*	*lest*	*seht*

You will notice that:

- all of their verb-**endings** are **regular**.

- the **vowel** in the verb-stem **changes** and only changes in the *du* and *er/sie/es/man* forms (i.e. 2nd and 3rd persons singular).

 Pass auf!

Verbs which already have an *-s* in the **infinitive** (e.g. *lesen, essen*) do **not** take an extra *-s* in the *-st* ending which belongs to the *du* form:

*ich le*se	*du lie*st	*er lie*st
*ich e*sse	*du i*sst	*sie i*sst

Toller Tipp!

Learn strong verbs like these **aloud** as soon as you first meet them. The sound-changes and sound-patterns will soon stick in your mind.

Your ears will soon pick up the major **patterns of vowel-changes**, like:

i.	*a → ä*	*ich fahre*	*du fährst*	*er fährt*	travel
		ich trage	*du trägst*	*sie trägt*	carry, wear
ii.	*e → i*	*ich esse*	*du isst*	*sie isst*	eat
		ich nehme	*du nimmst*	*man nimmt*	take
		ich helfe	*du hilfst*	*es hilft*	help
iii.	*e → ie*	*ich lese*	*du liest*	*er liest*	read
		ich sehe	*du siehst*	*er sieht*	see

You should note the **verb tables** of strong, modal and irregular verbs in Chapter 36, Appendix 1 for future reference. Once you have learnt the list of such verbs, any other verb you meet is predictably a regular weak verb: easy!

 # Fertig?

1 Was passt wozu?
Welche Antwort, rechts (A–J) passt zu welcher Frage, links (1–10)?

Which answer on the right (A–J) matches the question on the left (1–10)?

1. Was trägst du meistens am Wochenende?
2. Wie oft sehen Sie Ihre Familie?
3. Was isst du gern zum Abendessen?
4. Wo esst ihr alle zu Mittag?
5. Wie oft liest du die Zeitung?
6. Was für eine Schuluniform trägst du?
7. Wer fährt dich morgens in die Schule?
8. Spricht man Italienisch bei dir in Luzern?
9. Sprecht ihr oft Deutsch in der Deutschstunde?
10. Was siehst du am liebsten im Fernsehen?

A. Niemand fährt mich. Ich komme zu Fuß!
B. Ich sehe am liebsten Dokumentarfilme.
C. Ich lese keine Zeitung, nur Zeitschriften.
D. Ja, wir sprechen, hören und schreiben.
E. Am liebsten esse ich Tunfisch und Salat.
F. Nein! Wir sprechen nur Deutsch!
G. Ich trage eine Jacke und einen Schlips.
H. Ich sehe meine Familie nur abends.
I. Wir essen zusammen in der Kantine.
J. Ich trage gern ein T-Shirt und eine Jeans.

Grammatik Aktiv!

2 *Was fehlt?*

Fülle folgende Lücken mit Hilfe der unten angegebenen Verbformen im Präsens aus! Pass auf! Nicht alle Verbformen werden gebraucht!

Fill in the following gaps using verb-forms in the present, from the box below. Beware: not all are needed!

1. … wir mit dem Bus in die Stadt?
2. Das ist ein Foto von meiner Familie, … du?
3. Wann … Sie bitte meine Hausaufgaben?
4. … Sie, bitte, meine Reisetasche?
5. Hier … man kein Englisch!
6. … du oft deutsche Zeitschriften?
7. Wir … gern italienisch. Und du?
8. … man keine Schuluniform in Deutschland?
9. Meine Geschwister und ich … jeden Abend die Tophits im Fernsehen.
10. Meine Mutter … heute Abend ins Einkaufzentrum.

spricht	lesen	siehst	essen	trägt	fahren	tragen	liest	isst
tragt	sehen	fährt	fährst	siehst	fahre	sprecht		

H 3 *Lückentext*

Fülle folgende Lücken mit Hilfe der rechts angegebenen Infinitive -im Präsens- aus (siehe Kapitel 36, Appendix I)! Alle Verben, die nicht auf der Liste der starken, Modal-, bzw. unregelmäßigen Verben stehen, sind also regelmäßig.

Fill in the correct verb-forms of the infinitives given on the right, in the present tense. Refer to the appendix (Chapter 36). Any verbs not found in the strong/modal/irregular verb list are regular.

1. Die Schule … um acht Uhr.   beginnen
2. … es hier eine Bank in der Nähe?   geben
3. Was … du in der Hand?   halten
4. … du mir, bitte?   helfen
5. Ich nehme ein Vanilleeis. Was … du?   nehmen
6. Meine Eltern und ich … bis neun Uhr am Sonntag!   schlafen
7. Wann … ihr mit den Hausaufgaben fertig?   sein
8. Meine Mutter … das schnell in der Waschmaschine.   waschen
9. … du die Antwort auf diese Frage?   wissen
10. Was für eine Biersorte … Sie?   empfehlen

4 Bildertipps

Schreibe Sätze – mit Hilfe der in Kapiteln 15 und 16 gegebenen Beispiele –, die zu den folgenden Bildern passen!

With the help of examples from Chapters 15 and 16, write the sentences which best suit the following pictures.

 Los!

5 Ein Dialog voller Phantasie!

Schreibe einen Dialog mit einem Partner! Zuerst schreibt jeder 5 Fragen: z.B. 'Wo isst du dein Frühstück?' usw. Gib deinem Partner jetzt deine 5 Fragen! Jeder schreibt Antworten auf diese Fragen. Am Ende organisiert ihr alles in einem phantasiereichen Dialog.

Die besten Verben findet ihr vielleicht in der Verbtafel (siehe Kapitel 36, Appendix 1). Nimm jetzt diesen Dialog auf Kassette auf! Vergleiche ihn mit anderen aus der Klasse!

Write a dialogue with a partner. Each partner starts by writing 5 questions, e.g. 'Wo isst du dein Frühstück?' etc. You now give your partner your five questions and each of you write answers to these questions. Finally put these together into as imaginative a dialogue as possible.

You'll find the best verbs in the verb table (see Chapter 36, Appendix 1). You can then record it all on cassette and compare it with others from your class.

6 Wir … und ihr?

Schreibe (vielleicht mit einem Partner) einen Brief an eure deutschsprachige Partnerschule/Partnergesellschaft! Beschreibt einen typischen Schultag/Arbeitstag!

Beispiel:

> Der Unterricht beginnt um … Uhr. Wir haben … Stunden usw.
> Die Arbeit beginnt um … Uhr.

Nach jeder Aussage schreibt ihr eine passende Frage:

Beispiel:

> Wie viele Stunden habt ihr? Wie lange arbeiten Sie?

Wenn dieser Brief fertig ist, diskutiert ihr ihn mit einem Lehrer! Die Klasse könnte bzw. du könntest den besten Brief bzw. einen Artikel direkt per E-Mail an die deutschsprachigen Partner schicken!

Write a letter (perhaps with a partner) to your German-speaking partner (-school/company). Describe a typical day at school/work. Follow each statement with a relevant question on the same topic (see the examples above). When the letter is finished, discuss it with a teacher. You or your class could e-mail the best letter or article to your German-speaking partners.

GLOSSAR

das Einkaufszentrum	superstore, shopping centre
fertig sein	to have finished
empfehlen	to recommend
die Zeitung	newspaper
wissen	to know (a fact)

17

WE OUGHT TO, HE WANTS TO ...
modal verbs

 ## Auf die Plätze!

What is a modal verb?

The verbs *dürfen* (to be allowed to, may), *können* (to be able to, can), *mögen* (to like, like to), *müssen* (to have to, must), *sollen* (ought to, should), *wollen* (to want to) are called modal verbs. They are used to add extra information to what is already contained in a simple sentence, such as *ich schwimme*.

Beispiel:

Ich kann schwimmen	I am able to swim (= I can swim)
Ich will schwimmen	I want to swim
Ich muss schwimmen	I have to swim (= I must swim)

1 Modal verbs in German

Just as in English, German usually combines a modal verb with another verb, to form the whole sentence. Look carefully at these examples:

> Modal verb *wollen* –
> to want to. Agrees with *wir*

> Note that *zu* is not used
> before the infinitive

*Wir **wollen** morgen nach München **fahren**.*

> The infinitive of the basic verb
> *fahren* – to go, travel, is
> placed at the end of the clause.

We **want** to **travel** to Munich tomorrow.

*Er **muss** seine Hausaufgaben **machen**.*

He **has** (got) to **do** his homework.

> Modal verb *müssen* – to have
> to; must. Agrees with *er*

> The infinitive of the basic verb
> *schreiben* – to write, is placed at
> the end of the clause

Pass auf!

There are two things to remember when using modal verbs. First, don't forget to send the main verb to the end of the clause, and use it in its infinitive form. Second, you are normally told to put *zu* in front of an infinitive at the end of a clause. A sentence using a modal verb does not do this.

*Hast du etwas **zu** sagen?*   Have you something **to** say?
*Ich **möchte** ein Glas Cola trinken.*   I would **like to** drink a glass of Coke.

This is because the modal verbs, listed below, already have the idea of 'to' in them. If you add a *zu* in front of a modal, you are saying 'to' twice!

2 Modal verb forms

Modal verbs have some irregularities in their singular forms – *ich, du, er/sie/es* – but the pattern is simple to recognise.

	dürfen	*können*	*mögen*	*müssen*	*sollen*	*wollen*
	may	can	like	must	should	want
ich	*darf*	*kann*	*mag*	*muss*	*soll*	*will*
du	*darfst*	*kannst*	*magst*	*musst*	*sollst*	*willst*
er/sie/es	*darf*	*kann*	*mag*	*muss*	*soll*	*will*
wir	*dürfen*	*können*	*mögen*	*müssen*	*sollen*	*wollen*
ihr	*dürft*	*könnt*	*mögt*	*müsst*	*sollt*	*wollt*
sie/Sie	*dürfen*	*können*	*mögen*	*müssen*	*sollen*	*wollen*

 Toller Tipp!

Full tables of the modal verbs in all the tenses covered by this book can be found in Chapter 36.

3 Use of the modals
a Dürfen

■ Basic meaning 'to be allowed to' or 'may':

***Darf** ich heute bei Susi übernachten?*   **May** I spend the night at Susi's house?
*Sie **dürfen** hier nicht parken.*   You **may** not park here
(you're not **allowed to**).

b Können

■ **Basic meaning 'to be able to' or 'can':**

*Ich **kann** gut schwimmen.*	I **can** swim well.
*Maxi **kann** sehr gut Tennis spielen.*	Maxi plays/**can** play tennis very well.

■ **Sometimes the thing which you can do is unspoken in German:**

*Sabine **kann** gut Russisch (~~sprechen~~).*   Sabine **can** speak Russian well.

■ **Can imply possibility (sometimes using a subjunctive form – see Chapter 31 for more details):**

*Es **könnte** heute regnen.*   It **might (= could)** rain today.

 Pass auf!

The distinction between 'can' and 'may' is slowly disappearing, especially in spoken German:

***Darf** ich ein Eis haben?*	**May** I have an ice cream?
***Kann** ich ein Eis haben?*	**Can** I have an ice cream? [colloquial]

---

c Mögen

■ **Basic meaning 'to like':**

*Frank **mag keine** klassische Musik.*	Frank **doesn't** like classical music.
*Wir **mochten** unsere Austauschpartner sehr.*	We **liked** our exchange partners a lot.

■ **Can also indicate possibility:**

*Ja, das **mag** wohl sein.*   Yes, that **may/might** well be true.

■ **The subjunctive form möchte is a common way to say 'would like':**

*Ich **möchte** eine Zeitschrift kaufen.*   I **would like** to buy a magazine.

Toller Tipp!

If you want to use 'like' with another verb, e.g. to translate 'he likes to cook', use the construction *etwas gern(e) machen.*

Er kocht gerne.	He likes to cook (= he cooks gladly).
Sie gehen gern segeln.	They like to go sailing.

d Müssen

■ **Basic meaning 'to have to' or 'must':**

*Das Auto **muss** in die Werkstatt.**   The car **has to** go to the garage.
(*gehen is understood here)

■ **With *nicht* it can indicate choice, in the sense of 'need not', or 'don't have to':**

*Du **musst nicht** mitkommen.*   You **don't have to** come with us.
(NOT: You must not come with us)

Pass auf!

Note the distinction between 'must not/need not' (see above) and 'may not/not allowed':

*Heute **muss** ich **nicht** in die Schule gehen.*	I **don't have to** go to school today.
*Heute **darf** ich **nicht** in die Schule gehen.*	I am **not allowed** to go to school today.

e Sollen

■ **basic meaning 'ought to' or 'should/shall':**

*Um wie viel Uhr **sollen** wir uns treffen?*	What time **shall** we meet?
*Du **sollst** die Polizei anrufen!*	You are **supposed** to ring the police!

f Wollen

■ **Basic meaning 'to want to':**

> *Wir **wollten** schon seit langem kommen.*   We've **wanted** to come for a long time.

■ **It can indicate willingness, in the sense of 'let's...' or 'shall we.. ?'**

> ***Wollen** wir heute in eine Disko gehen?*   **Shall** we go to a disco tonight?

 Pass auf!

Remember that the German *will* **never** translates into the English future tense 'will':

> *Ich **will** den neuen James Bond   I **want to** see the new James
> Film sehen.*   Bond film.

Compare with:

> *Ich **werde** ihn mit meiner   I **will** see him with my girlfriend.
> Freundin sehen.*

4 Lassen

Although it is not a modal verb, *lassen* can be used in a very similar way. First of all, here are its present tense forms:

ich lasse	*wir lassen*
du lässt	*ihr lasst*
er/sie/es lässt	*sie/Sie lassen*

■ **Basic meanings 'to let', 'allow', 'leave':**

> *Ich habe eine CD bei dir **gelassen**.*   I **left** a CD at your house.
> ***Lass'** mich in Ruhe!*   **Leave** me alone!

■ **It can also translate – 'to have something done':**

> *Wir **lassen** einen Arzt kommen.*   We'll **get** a doctor to come.
> *Morgen **lasse** ich mein Haar schneiden.*   Tomorrow I'm **getting** my hair cut.

Fertig?

1 Wie spielt man 'Rugby'?

Ein deutscher Freund bzw. eine deutsche Freundin bittet dich, die Rugby Spielregeln zu erklären. Wähl ein Verb vom Kasten unten und trage es in eine Lücke ein!

A German friend asks you to explain the rules of rugby. Choose verbs from the box below, and fill in the gaps.

Eine Mannschaft … (1) fünfzehn Spieler auf dem Feld haben. Zwei Mannschaften … (2) gegeneinander spielen. Die Mannschaft, die die meisten Punkte bekommen … (3), gewinnt das Spiel. Die Spieler … (4) mit dem Ball laufen und … (5) versuchen, 'tries' zu machen, d.h. ein Spieler … (6) den Ball hinter die Linie der Gegner hinlegen. Jeder Spieler … (7) einen 'try' machen. Die anderen Spieler verteidigen ihre Linie und … (8) den Mann mit dem Ball körperlich abhalten. Rugby ist ein sehr hartes Spiel – ich … (9) es überhaupt nicht!

soll	müssen	sollen	kann	darf	mag	dürfen	will	dürfen

⊞ 2 Jens im Unglück

Dein Freund Jens war in letzter Zeit nicht sehr brav. Jetzt haben seine Eltern ihn dafür bestraft. Verwende die richtige Form des Verbs!

Recently, your friend Jens has not been very well-behaved. Now his parents have punished him. Use the correct form of the modal verb given in each sentence.

a. Er (sollen) zu Hause bleiben.
b. Seine Mutter (mögen) es nicht, wenn Jens die Schule schwänzt.
c. Jens (wollen) sein Schlafzimmer nicht aufräumen.
d. 'Du (müssen) in deinem Zimmer bleiben', sagt sie dazu.
e. Heute Abend (dürfen) Jens nicht mit seiner Freundin ins Kino gehen.
f. Seine Mutter sagt: 'Du (können) auch solange zu Hause bleiben, bis dein Zimmer wieder ordentlich ist!'

3 Was darfst du tun?

Du gehst in der Stadt einkaufen. Welches Modalverb passt zu den Bildern?

You have gone shopping in town. What is the correct modal verb for each picture?

1. **Beispiel:**

Der Polizist sagt: Hier *dürfen* Sie nicht parken.
wollen/mögen/dürfen

2.

Jens sagt: Ich ... ein Eis.

muss/soll/will

3.

Im Café sage ich: Vati, du ... nicht rauchen.
sollst/willst/magst

4.

Mutti sagt: ... wir heute Abend ins Kino?
dürfen/wollen/müssen

5.

Steffi sagt: Jens ... mir eine CD kaufen.
muss/mag/darf

6.

Der Verkäufer sagt: Es ... heute regnen. Haben Sie einen Regenschirm?
sollte/möchte/könnte

Grammatik Aktiv!

4 *Was ist die Lösung?*

Heute gibt es eine Menge Probleme. Verbinde die Probleme mit den richtigen Lösungen!

There are lots of problems today. Match up the problems with the right solutions.

1. Es ist mir kalt.
2. Es regnet.
3. Herr Frenssens Auto hat eine Panne.
4. Ich habe viel Hausaufgaben zu machen.
5. Stefan hat sein Taschengeld verloren.
6. Wir langweilen uns.
7. Tante Beate bäckt eine Torte.
8. Ich muss zur Bank.

a. Wir müssen mit dem Bus zur Schule fahren.
b. Dürfen wir vielleicht zur Schwimmhalle?
c. Er will es wieder finden.
d. Luzie will sie gerne essen.
e. Mit dem Computer kann ich das schneller tun.
f. Es muss in die Werkstatt.
g. Möchtest du mitkommen?
h. Du solltest die Heizung anschalten.

◫ 5 *E-Mail aus Deutschland*

Du erhältst eine E-Mail-Nachricht von einer Freundin in Deutschland, aber die Nachricht ist irgendwie durcheinander geraten. Entziffere die in kursiv geschriebenen Zeilen!

You have received an e-mail from a friend in Germany, but somehow it has got all jumbled up. Unjumble the lines in italics to decipher the whole message.

Hallo nochmals! Wie geht es dir? Mir geht es ganz gut :-) Bitte grüße mal deine Eltern. (1) *deinen Bruder auch du grüßen von mir sollst.*
Habt ihr die neue CD von den BadBoyz gehört? Sie ist ganz toll. (2) *CD diese anhören ihr solltet.* Bald habe ich Geburtstag. (3) *kann kaufen dann vielleicht die CD ich.* (4) *einen Geburtstag Computer zum ich möchte.* (5) *was du zum willst Geburtstag?*
(6) *Onkel Frank mein auswandern Kanada und seine Frau wollen nach.* Sie werden mir sehr fehlen :-((7) *können meine Französisch beide Kusinen schon sehr gut.* (8) *Jetzt sie Englisch auch müssen lernen.*
(9) *wie viel Uhr du ins Bett musst um gehen?* (10) *10.30 Uhr ich bleiben bis abends wach darf.*
(11) *ist Das alles, was ich dir kann erzählen zur Zeit.* Ich wünsche dir alles Gute –

Bis bald,
:-) :-) Uschi :-) :-)

Los!

6 Wie komme ich am besten zu dir?

*Beschreibe einem Freund den Weg vom Bahnhof zu deinem Haus! Vergiss nicht, die Modalverben zu verwenden: **du sollst …, du kannst …** usw!*

Describe to a friend how s/he can find the way from the station to your house. Don't forget to use modal verb forms: **you should …, you can…** etc.

7 Erklär' es nochmal! (siehe Übung 2)

Schreibe zehn Sätze, die die Spielregeln einer Sportart oder eines Brettspieles erklären! Oder du könntest dein Lieblingsrezept beschreiben. Jeder Satz sollte ein Modalverb haben.

Write ten sentences which explain the rules of a sport or board game. Or you can describe your favourite recipe. Each sentence should use a modal verb.

GLOSSAR

übernachten	to spend the night
die Schule schwänzen	to skip classes/to skive off school
verteidigen	to defend
auswandern	to emigrate
segeln	to sail
sich benehmen	to behave
körperlich	physical(ly)
verbringen	to spend (time)
staubsaugen	to hoover
aufräumen	to clear up

18

I WILL GO, SHE WILL STUDY
future tense

**Auf die Plätze!**

What is the future tense?
You use this tense to talk about things which will happen at some point in the future:

> *Wir werden nach Stuttgart fahren.* We will go to Stuttgart.

1 Formation
German uses the present tense forms of *werden*, plus the basic (or infinitive) form of the main verb. Look at these examples:

> *Wir **werden** dich bald **besuchen**.* We**'ll visit** you soon.
> *Ich **werde** ins Kino **gehen**, wenn ich* I**'ll go** to the cinema, if I've the time.
> *Zeit habe.*

Whatever verb you use in the future, it is only ever the form of *werden* which changes to agree with the subject. The main verb never changes from its infinitive. Look how the verb *gehen* is conjugated in the future tense:

> *gehen* – to go *ich **werde** gehen* *wir **werden** gehen*
>   *du **wirst** gehen* *ihr **werdet** gehen*
>   *er **wird** gehen*   *sie/Sie **werden** gehen*

> Use the right (present tense) form of *werden*

> *Wir **werden** morgen darüber **sprechen**.* We'll talk about it tomorrow.

> You don't need to put *zu* in front of the infinitive

114

2 Talking about the future without *werden*

Like English, German sometimes uses a present tense verb to indicate an action which is quite obviously in the future. This is usually because words like *morgen* (tomorrow), or *nächstes Jahr* (next year) etc. are being used.

*Ich gehe **morgen** einkaufen.*	I'm going shopping **tomorrow**.
***Nächstes Jahr** fahren wir nach Amerika.*	We're going to America **next year**.

■ Where the future tense **is** used, it can emphasise the difference between an action or event in the present and the future:

Das nächste Mal werden wir besser spielen.	We'll play better next time.

■ Or it can simply emphasise the future event:

*Was **werde** ich nun machen?*	What **will/shall** I do now?

 Pass auf!

The German word *will* is a false friend. *Will* means 'want to' and is a modal verb. See Chapter 17 for more details.

*Ich **werde** diese Sendung sehen.*	I **will** watch this programme.
*Ich **will** diese Sendung sehen.*	I **want to** watch this programme.

 # Fertig?

1 Wechseln, bitte!
Schreibe die untenstehenden Verben im Futur!

Write the verb forms below in the future tense.

1. ich komme
2. wir singen
3. du schläfst
4. Sie sehen
5. er lernt

6. Wir gehen einkaufen.
7. Ich mache meine Hausaufgaben.
8. Markus und seine Schwester besuchen ihren Opa.
9. Petra sieht in ihrem Zimmer fern.
10. Kommt ihr mit?

2 Wie sieht die Zukunft aus?

Die folgenden Sätze beschreiben, wie Karls Zukunft aussieht. Bring die Wörter in die richtige Reihenfolge!

The following sentences describe what Karl's future looks like. Rewrite the sentences in the correct order.

1. werde machen mein ich Abitur.
2. leisten meinen ich Zivildienst ab werde.
3. werde ich dann studieren an der Englisch Universität.
4. ich eine finden werde Stelle.
5. werde Frau eine schöne heiraten ich.
6. Kinder ich und werden viele bekommen meine Frau.

⊞ 3 Ab in die Sonne

Welche Länder werden diese Personen im kommenden Sommer besuchen? Fülle die Lücken aus!

Which countries will these people visit for their summer holidays? Fill in the gaps.

1. Herr und Frau Müller … nach Mallorca fliegen.
2. Petra Klein … ihre Tante in Großbritannien besuchen.
3. Ich … auf den Mond fliegen!
4. Die Familie Grün … zwei Wochen lang durch Amerika fahren.
5. Sag mal, Thomas, … du wieder nach Frankreich fahren?
6. Wohin … Sie in Urlaub reisen, Frau Siemens? – Mein Mann und ich … nach Monaco fahren.

⊞ 4 Pläne, planen

Diese Leute haben in den kommenden Tagen vieles vor. Was werden sie alle machen?

These people have lots of plans for the next few days. What will they do?

1. Oma

2. Stefan

3. Herr Graf

4. Sandra und Gerd

5. Tante Petra

6. Ich

Los!

5 Ein frohes Neujahr!

Ein neues Jahr fängt an! Du kannst einen neuen Anfang machen. Schreibe einen Brief an einen deutschen Freund: Welche guten Vorsätze hast du? Vergiss nicht, im Futur zu schreiben!

It's the start of a New Year and you can make a fresh start. Write a letter to a German friend about your resolutions. Don't forget to use the future tense!

Beispiel:

Für dieses Jahr habe ich mir fest vorgenommen:
– Ich werde weniger Schokolade essen.
– Ich werde nie mehr mit meinen Freunden streiten.

⊞ 6 Im Jahre 3000

Stell dir mal das Leben im Jahre 3000 vor! Wie werden die Städte aussehen? Welche Musik wird man hören? Gib deiner Phantasie freien Lauf! Du solltest mindestens zehn Sätze schreiben.

Try to imagine life in the year 3000. What will the cities look like? What kind of music will people listen to? Let your imagination run riot! Write at least ten sentences.

GLOSSAR

einkaufen	to shop
die Sendung	a programme, broadcast
die Zukunft	future
das Abitur	German equivalent to A levels
der Zivildienst	civilian service (an alternative for young German men who don't want to do their compulsory military service)
die Stelle	job
heiraten	to marry
der Mond	moon
etwas vorhaben	to have plans
stricken	to knit
der gute Vorsatz	good resolution

19

HAVE YOU SEEN?

perfect tense

 **Auf die Plätze!**

What is the perfect tense?

The perfect tense is commonly used to talk about something which has already happened.

1 Forming the perfect tense in German

To form this tense in German you need the **present tense form of *haben* (or sometimes *sein* –** see below), which acts as the **auxiliary** (from the Latin word meaning 'to help', the auxiliary helps you form other tenses), plus the **past participle** of the verb concerned:

> The auxiliary should agree with the subject *wir*.

*Wir **haben** Tennis **gespielt**.*   We played tennis.

> The past participle is placed at the end of the clause.

2 Auxiliary haben or sein?

A number of verbs do not use *haben* as their auxiliary verb, but *sein*. If you have done some French, you might recognize the categories which do this, but even if you haven't, the following rules will help you to decide which auxiliary verb to use:

■ many verbs of motion (come, go, run, fall etc.):

> e.g. *fahren*
> *Er **ist** nach Hause gefahren.*   He has gone home.

■ verbs which imply a change of state:

> e.g. *einschlafen*
> *Ich **bin** schnell eingeschlafen.*   I quickly fell asleep.

> e.g. *sterben*
> *Sie **ist** gestorben.*   She (has) died.

■ the following:

> *werden*
> *Stefan **ist** Polizist geworden.*   Stefan has become a policeman.

> *sein*
> *Wir **sind** krank gewesen.*   We have been ill.

3 Forming the past participle

The past participle (English 'played', 'talked' etc.) always shows that we are looking at a past tense. All regular German verbs follow the same pattern of **ge** + stem + **t** ending:

wohnen	**ge**woh**nt**	lived
machen	**ge**mac**ht**	made, did
fragen	**ge**frag**t**	asked
sagen	**ge**sag**t**	said

A few regular verbs do not add the *ge-* to the front, simply because it would be awkward to say the word if you did! This is because they already begin with *be-*, *er-*, *ver-*, *ent*:

besuchen	*besuch**t***	visited
erzählen	*erzähl**t***	told

4 Irregular past participles

Some verbs have strong or irregular past participles. These tend to do one or more of three things:

- ■ they **might** not add the *ge-* in front of the stem;

- ■ the vowel in the stem might add an umlaut, or change altogether; and

- ■ the majority keep the **-en** ending.

so:

kennen	*ge**ka**nnt*	knew
fahren	**ge***fahren*	went
beginnen	*beg**o**nnen*	began
trinken	**ge***tr**u**nken*	drunk
bleiben	**ge***bl**ie**ben*	stayed

Toller Tipp!

For a full list of verbs with irregular past participles or which use *sein* to form the past tenses, see Chapter 36, Appendix 1.

Fertig?

1 Was haben sie heute Morgen gemacht?
Fülle die Lücken aus, um einen Satz zu bilden, der die Abbildung beschreibt!

Fill in the gaps to create a phrase which describes the activity in the picture.

1. Ich … mir die Zähne …

2. Herr Reuter … mit dem Zug …

3. Wir … Tischtennis …

4. Du … im Schwimmbad …

5. Charley und Lisbeth … den Tisch …

2 Am Wochenende
Welches Partizip passt zu welchem Satz?

Which participle goes with which sentence?

1. Ich bin um zehn Uhr …
2. Um zehn Uhr dreißig habe ich mein Frühstück …
3. Um elf Uhr haben meine Freunde und ich Fußball …
4. Am Nachmittag bin ich mit meinem Bruder zum Zoo …
5. Nach dem Abendessen bin ich schnell … , weil ich sehr müde war.

| aufgestanden | gespielt | eingeschlafen | gegessen | gegangen |

3 Ich habe schon alles gemacht
Setze ins Perfekt!

Put the following into the perfect tense.

1. Was denkst du.
2. Wir helfen dir.
3. Er findet -20, -DM.
4. Wissen Sie?
5. Das weiß ich.
6. Ich komme nach Hause.
7. Sie schläft bis 10 Uhr.
8. Wir sind im Kino.
9. Er liegt im Krankenhaus.
10. Er wohnt in Berlin.

🄷 4 Das fünfte Rad
Welches Partizip passt nicht in die Reihe? Bilde mit diesem einen Satz!

Which past participle is the odd one out? Make up a sentence with it.

Beispiel:

(gekommen) gemacht gefunden geschlafen gehört
Oma ist am Freitag gekommen.

(*gekommen* is the odd one out as it is the only one which uses *sein* as its auxiliary).

1. gehört gelaufen gewohnt gesehen gegessen
2. vergessen gekauft gelernt besucht gekostet
3. gekommen gestorben gefahren gewesen genommen
4. gesagt gekauft gesehen verletzt gelebt
5. gesprungen geholfen gemacht getragen geblieben

 Los!

5 Die Sommerferien
Beschreibe einem Freund deine Ferien im letzten Sommer! Was hast du besucht? Was hast du gemacht? Bist du dorthin geflogen? usw.

Describe your last summer holiday to a friend. Where did you go? What did you do? Did you fly there? etc.

Grammatik Aktiv!

⊞ 6 Erzähl weiter!

Lies den untenstehenden Satz! Versuch, die Geschichte Satz für Satz weiterzuerzählen (alleine oder mit Freunden)!

Read the sentence below. Try to continue the story, sentence by sentence (either on your own or with friends).

> Gestern bin ich in die Stadt gegangen. Dort habe ich etwas ganz Merkwürdiges gesehen ...

GLOSSAR

einschlafen	to fall asleep
das fünfte Rad am Wagen sein	to be the odd one out
sterben	to die
der Satz	sentence
merkwürdig	strange, weird

20

SIT YOURSELVES DOWN!
reflexive verbs

 **Auf die Plätze!**

What is a reflexive verb?
There are certain activities which we normally associate with the words 'myself',
'yourself', 'himself' etc., such as 'John washes himself' or 'I have hurt myself'.
These are known as **reflexive verbs**. This is where the action of the verb seems to
reflect back on the person doing it.

1 Formation of reflexive verbs
Reflexive verbs in German only differ from normal verbs by the use of **the reflexive
pronouns** (in English 'myself' etc.). So *waschen* ('to wash') becomes *sich waschen* ('to
wash **oneself**').

ich wasche	+	*mich*	I wash **myself**
du wäschst	+	*dich*	you wash **yourself**
er wäscht	+	*sich*	he washes **himself**
wir waschen	+	*uns*	we wash **ourselves**
ihr wascht	+	*euch*	you wash **yourselves**
sie/Sie waschen	+	*sich*	they wash **themselves**/you wash **yourself**

(Note that the above are the *accusative* forms of the reflexive pronoun *sich*. Below we
will look at verbs using the *dative* form.)

 Pass auf!

The reflexive pronoun is placed as close to the verb as possible:

*Lisbeth **interessiert sich** sehr*   Lisbeth is very **interested** in ballet.
für Ballett.

---

*Wir **freuen uns** sehr auf die Ferien.*	We are really **looking forward** to the holidays.
*Darf ich **mich vorstellen?***	May I **introduce myself?**

There are more reflexive verbs in German than in English. In the examples above, 'to be interested in' and 'to look forward to' do not seem to be reflexive, yet the German equivalents still need a reflexive pronoun.

2 Verbs which suggest actions you do to yourself

sich aufregen	to get excited	*sich waschen*	to wash (oneself)
sich anziehen	to get dressed	*sich vorstellen*	to introduce oneself
sich ausziehen	to get undressed	*sich bewegen*	to move (oneself)
sich umziehen	to get changed	*sich beeilen*	to hurry (oneself)
sich rasieren	to shave (oneself)	*sich setzen*	to sit down
sich entschuldigen	to excuse oneself, to apologise	*sich duschen*	to shower

3 Verbs which suggest actions you do to each other

sich treffen	to meet one another	*sich kennen*	to know each other
sich schlagen	to hit each other	*sich streiten*	to argue with each other
sich lieben	to love each other		

4 Verbs where the English equivalent doesn't seem to be reflexive at all

sich freuen auf	to look forward to	*sich interessieren für*	to be interested in
sich erkälten	to catch a cold	*sich erholen*	to get better
sich verlaufen	to get lost	*sich ereignen*	to happen
sich befinden	to be (in a place)	*sich entscheiden*	to decide
sich erinnern	to remember		

5 Dative reflexive pronouns

The verb *sich vorstellen* (to introduce oneself) has an alternative meaning, 'to imagine', but then uses the dative form of the reflexive pronoun, as shown below:

*ich stelle **mir** vor*	I imagine
*du stellst **dir** vor*	you imagine
*er/sie stellt **sich** vor*	he/she imagines
*wir stellen **uns** vor*	we imagine
*ihr stellt **euch** vor*	you imagine
*sie/Sie stellen **sich** vor*	they/you imagine

■ In addition, many of the verbs in sections 2–4 are forced to use dative pronouns if you introduce another object, e.g the thing which you are washing. This is actually done to avoid confusion and make it quite clear which thing is the object of the washing. Look at the difference between these two examples:

*Ich wasche **mich** im Badezimmer.*   I wash (**myself**) in the bathroom.
*Ich wasche **mir** die Hände.*   I wash **my hands**.

> Because *die Hände* is already an **accusative** direct object, we have to use *mir*, which is a **dative** reflexive pronoun. This makes it clear that the hands are being washed.

Fertig?

1 Was sagen sie?
Setze das passende Pronomen ein!

Insert the appropriate reflexive pronoun.

1. Thorsten und Arndt sagen:

Wir haben _____ geschlagen.

2. Herr Hubner, mein Lehrer, sagt:

Setz _____, bitte!

Grammatik Aktiv!

3. Vati sagt:

Ich möchte _____ rasieren.

4. Lotte fragt die Touristin:

Haben Sie _____ verlaufen?

5. Petra und Dirk sagen:

Wir lieben _____ sehr.

6. Vor dem Abendessen sagt Mutter:

Ich muss _____ die Hände waschen.

7. Der Arzt sagt:

Ich glaube, Hanna hat _____ erkältet.

mich
mir
dich
sich
uns
uns
sich

2 Fragen und Antworten

Beantworte die Fragen mit der in Klammern geschriebenen Information!

Answer the questions, using the words in brackets.

Beispiel:

> Womit wäscht sich Vati? [er   mit Seife]
>
> Er wäscht sich mit Seife.

1. Worauf freust du dich, Karl? [ich   auf den Geburtstag]
2. Wie lange kennt ihr euch? [wir   seit zwei Jahren]
3. Wofür interessieren Sie sich, Frau Hein? [ich   für Kunst]
4. Wo treffen wir uns? [wir   vor dem Kino]
5. Wo befindet sich dein Haus? [es   in der Klarastraße]

⊞ 3 Wie mein Tag anfängt

Wie sieht dein Tag aus? Fülle die Lücken aus, aber pass gut auf: nicht alle Verben sind reflexiv! Die richtigen Verben kannst du unten finden.

What is your day like? Fill in the gaps, but watch out: not all the verbs you will need are reflexive. The infinitives of the verbs you need are below.

Um sieben Uhr   ….   Um diese Zeit   ….   mein Vater im Badezimmer. Wenn das Badezimmer frei ist,   ….   Dann   ….   (normalerweise eine Jeans-Hose und ein T-Shirt), bevor ich nach unten gehe. In der Küche   ….   an den Tisch, wo ich dann mein Frühstück   ….   Um acht Uhr   ….   ich das Haus und gehe zur Bushaltestelle. Da meine Schule nicht sehr weit weg ist,   ….   oft dorthin zu Fuß zu gehen. Wenn es aber regnet,   ….   ganz froh, mit dem Bus fahren zu können!

Reflexive verbs:

sich entscheiden   sich anziehen   sich duschen   sich rasieren   sich setzen

Other verbs:

sein   aufstehen   verlassen   essen

Los!

4 Kennt ihr euch schon?

Schreibe eine Liste von Fragen, um dadurch deinen neuen Brieffreund bzw. deine Brieffreundin besser kennenzulernen! Schreibe auch deine Antworten auf!

Write a list of questions, so that you can get to know your new pen pal better. Write answers to the questions about yourself.

Beispiel:

> Wofür interessierst du dich?
> Ich interessiere mich sehr für Musik.

GLOSSAR

sich schlagen	to fight each other
aufstehen	to get up
die Seife	soap
die Bushaltestelle	bus stop

21

THE TRAIN NOW DEPARTING ...
separable and inseparable verbs

 ## Auf die Plätze!

What are separable and inseparable verbs?
The meanings of many German verbs: *kommen, fahren, machen* etc. can be changed
by adding prefixes – words or groups of letters – to the front of the verb. Some of
these prefixes are separable, and can detach themselves from their 'host verb', while
others have to stay with the verb at all times (inseparable).

1 Separable verbs
The prefix of separable verbs is often a preposition like *an, ab, mit, aus, zu* etc. In a
dictionary these verbs are usually distinguished by the use of (*sep.*) or a dash between
the verb and the prefix e.g. ***mit-kommen***. In most cases, the new meaning of the
verb is based on the root verb, but this is not always the case.

kommen	to come	→	*an-kommen*	to arrive
machen	to make	→	*zu-machen*	to close (make shut)
lesen	to read	→	*vor-lesen*	to read out loud
But:				
ziehen	to pull	→	*um-ziehen*	to change (clothes); to move (house)

2 Position of the separable prefix
If the prefix can separate from its verb, where does it go? In the majority of cases,
the prefix goes to the end of the clause or sentence:

> *Der Zug **fährt** um zwei Uhr von Gleis 6 **ab**.*
> The train **departs** at 2 o'clock from platform 6.

If you use one of these verbs in its infinitive form (with a different verb at the start
of the sentence), the verb is sent to the end as well (see Chapter 1 on word order),
and it and the prefix are reunited:

*Willst du morgen **mitkommen**?*
Do you want to **come with us** tomorrow?

This is also the case when you form the past participle of these verbs (see Chapter 19), because past participles are sent to the end of the clause too. Just remember that the *ge-* goes between the prefix and the verb:

*Herr Schröder hat die Tür **zugemacht**.*
Herr Schröder has **closed** the door.

Finally, if you use the infinitive with *zu*, this also goes between the prefix and the verb:

*Christine hat sich entschieden, nicht **mitzukommen**.*
Christine has decided not to come with us.

3 Inseparable verbs

Some prefixes, which seem to be separable, are not: verbs beginning with *be-, emp-, ent-, er-, ge-, miss-, ver-, zer-* cannot be split. Some dictionaries might remind you of this by putting *(insep.)* or a similar indication next to the verb. These verbs are also less likely to have a recognisable link to the root verb.

bekommen	to receive, get	*entkommen*	to escape
empfehlen	to recommend	*befehlen*	to order/command
zerstören	to destroy	*verstören*	to distress

Needless to say, these verbs never separate, and are no different to any other standard German verb. *Zu*, when it is used, comes before the verb, and the past participle is not affected (in fact, all these verbs are strong, and do not have *ge-* at the start).

Toller Tipp!

You might find it useful to remember:

ohne … zu …   without …
um … zu …   in order to …

These constructions are always found within a subordinate (secondary) clause. Therefore, the infinitive verb is sent to the end of the sentence (ie. after the … *zu* …):
*Er geht, **ohne** es ihr **zu** sagen* (he leaves without telling her);
*Ich brauche Hilfe, **um** meine Hausaufgaben **zu** machen* (I need help in order to do my homework).

NB When this construction is used with a separable verb, the ... *zu* ... is placed between the prefix and the verb, e.g.,
Ich brauche deine Telefonnummer, **um** *dich* **an**zu*rufen* (I need your phone number in order to call you);
Ich schaute, **ohne** *mit*zu*machen* (I looked without joining in).

4 Prefixes which can be separable and inseparable!

A very small number of prefixes can be both separable and inseparable! Common ones are *durch-*, *über-*, *um-*, *unter-*, *voll-*, *wieder-*. Some of these verbs have a totally different meaning depending on whether their prefix is separable or inseparable. Thus:

inseparable prefix		separable prefix	
übersetzen	to translate	*über-setzen*	to transfer
durchreisen	to travel all over	*durch-reisen*	to travel through

Letztes Jahr haben wir ganz Europa **durchreist**.
We **travelled all over** Europe last year.
Wir sind in drei Tagen durch Deutschland **durchgereist**.
We **crossed** Germany in three days.

 Pass auf!

Don't treat these verbs, whether separable or inseparable, differently when forming the different tenses. *Abfahren*, for example, is formed the same way as *fahren*, it's just that there's an extra bit to think about. **Check** the different forms in a dictionary, or at the back of this book, if you're not sure.

5 Hin- and her-

The two separable prefixes *hin-* and *her-* are particularly common. They indicate motion towards or away from the speaker or the subject of a sentence. Look at these examples:

Meine Schwester ist gestern **her**gekommen.
My sister came here yesterday (i.e. to us).

Letztes Jahr bin ich nach Deutschland **hin**gefahren.
Last year I travelled to Germany (i.e. away from here).

You will come across them in some important commands, too.

Gib's mal her!	Give it to me!
Bitte, setzt euch hin!	Please, sit down (over there)!
Herein!	Come in!
Gehen Sie ruhig hinein!	Do go in!

 # Fertig?

1 Aussteigen – steigen aus
Entferne die Modalverben, dann schreibe die Sätze mit den trennbaren Verben!

Remove the modal verbs then rewrite using the separable verbs.

Beispiel:

> Vati musste die Tür aufmachen. → Vati machte die Tür auf.

1. Ich möchte am Hauptbahnhof aussteigen.
2. Der Zug soll um 14.27 Uhr abfahren.
3. Wir sollen unsere Hausaufgaben anfangen.
4. Willst du bitte deine Geschichte weitererzählen?
5. Die Lehrerin sagt: Ihr müsst das Gedicht vorlesen.

H 2 Die Qual der Wahl
Du musst dich entscheiden, ob diese Verben trennbar oder untrennbar sind. Wenn sie doch trennbar sind, schreibe die Sätze neu!

Decide if these verbs are separable or not, then rewrite the sentences if a verb is separable.

1. Die Studenten (wiederholen) den Satz.
2. Ute (umsteigen) in Köln.
3. Thomas (hinfahren).
4. (Übersetzen) Sie ins Englische, bitte schön!
5. Ich hoffe, wir (wiedersehen) uns bald.

Los!

3 Verbinden und Trennen

Unten kannst du eine Liste von Vorsilben sehen. Mit einem Wörterbuch finde so viele Verben wie du kannst, die diese Vorsilben benutzen!

Below is a list of prefixes. Find as many verbs as possible in a dictionary, which use them.

aus	hin	voll	kennen	unter

Beispiel:

>   aus-steigen

4 Verbinden und Trennen (2)

Schreibe Sätze mit den Verben, die du in Übung 3 gefunden hast!

Write sentences with the verbs you found in Exercise 3.

Beispiel:

>   Herr Ludsen steigt in Hamburg aus.

GLOSSAR

trennen	to separate
(un)trennbar	(in)separable
die Vorsilbe	prefix
abfahren	to depart
wegen	because of
die Geschichte	story
das Gedicht	poem
vorlesen	to read out loud
die Qual der Wahl	(lit.) the agony of choice
verbinden	to join together

22

I, THEY AND WE; ME, THEM & US
pronouns

 **Auf die Plätze!**

What are pronouns?
Every noun can be replaced by a pronoun.

> *Frau Stein* gab *den Studenten*
> *Hausaufgaben auf.*
> *Ich habe* **einen Wagen** *gekauft.*

> *Sie gab* **ihnen** *viel zu tun.*

> *Er hat 6000,-DM gekostet.*

1 Nominative pronouns

Use these pronouns to replace a person or thing which is the **subject** of a sentence or clause.

ich	I	*wir*	we
du	you (familiar singular)	*ihr*	you (familiar plural)
er	he	*sie*	they
sie	she	*Sie*	you (polite)
es	it		

These pronouns are most commonly used before a verb, instead of the name of a person or thing:

> **Marco** *wohnt in München.* **Er** *ist aber Italiener.*
> **Marco** lives in Munich. But **he** is Italian.

2 Accusative pronouns

Use these pronouns when the person or thing to be replaced is the **direct object.**

mich	me	*uns*	us
dich	you (familiar singular)	*euch*	you (familiar plural)
ihn	him	*sie*	them
sie	her	*Sie*	you (polite)
es	it		

*Er liebt **mich**!*   He loves **me**!

*Wir treffen **sie** um achtzehn Uhr.*   We're meeting **them** at six this evening.

*Ralf hat einen Plan von Dresden. Er hat **ihn** an einer Tankstelle gekauft.*
Ralf has a map of Dresden. He bought **it** in a petrol station.

3 Dative pronouns

Use these pronouns when the person or thing is the **indirect object**.

mir	(to) me	*uns*	(to) us
dir	(to) you	*euch*	(to) you
ihm	(to) him	*ihnen*	(to) them
ihr	(to) her	*Ihnen*	(to) you
ihm	(to) it		

*Wie geht es **dir**?*   How are **you**?

*Es gab einen Streit zwischen **ihnen**.*   There was an argument between **them**.

*Die Katze schläft unter dem Tisch. Sie schläft oft unter **ihm**.*
The cat is sleeping under the table. She often sleeps under **it.**

(See Section 5, below, for a more useful way of saying this sentence.)

 Pass auf!

> You might have noticed in the examples given above that pronoun forms are affected by prepositions just like the nouns they replace.
>
> *Ich spiele Fußball mit **meinen Freunden**. Ich spiele mit **ihnen**.*

4 Order of pronouns

German pronouns should be written in the following order:

i. **Subject** ii. **Direct object** iii. **Indirect object**
(nominative) (accusative) (dative)

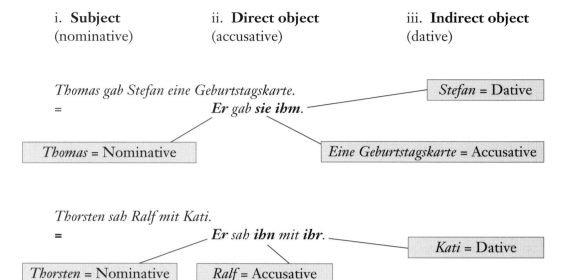

Thomas gab Stefan eine Geburtstagskarte.
=   *Er gab **sie ihm**.*

Stefan = Dative	
Thomas = Nominative	*Eine Geburtstagskarte* = Accusative

Thorsten sah Ralf mit Kati.
=   *Er sah **ihn** mit **ihr**.*

Thorsten = Nominative	*Kati* = Dative
Ralf = Accusative	

If you have a mix of pronoun and noun objects, the pronoun will come first.

Ich gebe meinem Bruder einen Apfel.	I give my brother an apple.
*Ich gebe **ihm** einen Apfel.*	I give him an apple.
*Ich gebe **ihn** meinem Bruder.*	I give it to my brother.

5 Prepositions with pronouns

We have already noted that pronouns can be affected by prepositions. With many prepositions you can put **da-** (or **dar-**) in front of them to replace the object pronoun altogether.

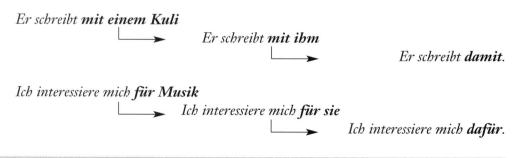

*Er schreibt **mit einem Kuli***
    ⟶   *Er schreibt **mit ihm***
         ⟶   *Er schreibt **damit**.*

*Ich interessiere mich **für Musik***
    ⟶   *Ich interessiere mich **für sie***
         ⟶   *Ich interessiere mich **dafür**.*

 ### Toller Tipp!

You will also find all the German pronouns in a table at the back of this book. See Chapter 37.

Fertig?

1 Suchrätsel
Alle Pronomen sind irgendwo im Worträtsel versteckt – außer einem. Welches fehlt?

All the pronouns are hidden somewhere within this wordsearch – except for one. Which one is missing?

M	I	H	R	B	D	Y	I	H	N
I	A	P	B	Q	H	T	G	M	Y
C	S	I	C	H	N	D	K	I	I
H	S	I	E	D	E	E	L	R	H
M	J	Z	X	I	N	S	P	V	M
I	B	E	A	C	P	W	Y	M	J
H	D	P	L	H	J	G	F	S	Q
R	I	U	W	I	R	W	Z	D	U
K	R	N	X	A	U	E	U	C	H
T	F	S	I	H	E	R	M	N	O

2 Frohe Weihnachten
Wer bekommt dieses Jahr welches Geschenk? Mach eine Liste nach dem Beispiel unten! Alle Pronomen, die du brauchst, findest du im Kasten.

Who's going to get which present from you this Christmas? Write a present list, following the example below. All the pronouns you need are in the box.

Beispiel:

Ich schenke Onkel Frank einen Hut.   Ich schenke *ihn ihm.*

Geschenke
eine Flasche Whisky

Personen
~~Onkel Frank~~

Grammatik Aktiv!

eine Wärmeflasche

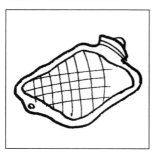

Opa

Socken

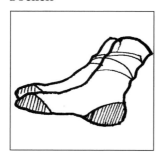

Mutti

ein Gummimäuschen

Oma

~~einen Hut~~

Mietze

einen Schal

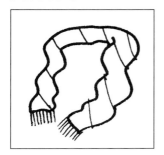

Vati

einen Reiseatlas

Tante Dora

sie   ~~ihn~~   ihm   sie   ihn   es   ~~ihm~~   ihm   ihr   sie   ihr   ihn
ihr   ihm   ihn   ihr

H 3 Bericht eines Besuches

Robert hat einen Bericht über seinen Deutschlandbesuch geschrieben. Du musst den Bericht mit den richtigen Pronomen vervollständigen.

Robert has written a report of his visit to Germany. You have to complete the account by adding the correct pronouns.

Vor zwei Wochen habe ich meinen Brieffreund Erich in Kiel besucht. (He) … war ganz nett zu (me) … . (I) … habe mich sehr gefreut, (him) … endlich besuchen zu können, weil (I) … seit zwei Jahren mit (him) … im Briefwechsel stehe. (I) … war drei Wochen lang bei (him) … .

Seine Familie war eigentlich auch total nett. Sein Vater ist Bankangestellter und arbeitet im Zentrum von Kiel. (He) … kam jeden Abend sehr spät nach Hause und (I) … habe (him) … während der Woche nicht sehr oft gesehen. Seine Mutter ist Lehrerin. (She) … war oft zu Hause und (I) … habe sehr viel mit (her) … gesprochen. (She) … hat (us) … die ganze Stadt gezeigt. Erich hat auch eine ältere

Schwester, aber (she) … ist schon verheiratet und lebt mit ihrem Mann in Hamburg. (I) … habe (them) … gar nicht gesehen.

Kiel war wunderschön. (It) … ist eine sehr schöne Hafenstadt im Norden von Deutschland. Der Hafen ist sehr groß – es gibt dort viele große Segelboote und Jachten zu sehen. Ich fand (them) … alle sehr, sehr schön.

Der Besuch war wirklich ganz toll. Erich hat (me) … nächstes Jahr nochmals eingeladen – (I) … freue (myself) … sehr darauf.

Los!

4 Ärger mit den Eltern
Deine Eltern geben dir viele Aufgaben. Welche Aufgaben musst du noch tun? Sage, dass du alles später erledigen wirst.

Your parents have plenty of jobs for you to do. Which jobs do you still have to finish? Say that you'll do them later, using the correct pronoun for each activity.

Beispiele:

Du sollst dein Zimmer aufräumen.	OK, ich räume es morgen auf.
Hast du deine Hausaufgaben schon fertig?	Ich mache sie heute Abend fertig.
Spiel mit deinem Bruder!	Ja, ja, ich spiele später mit *ihm*.

⊞ 5 Zeitungsdeutsch
Lies einen deutschen Zeitungsartikel! Finde alle Pronomen und schreibe sie, mit dem dazugehörigen Substantiv, auf ein Blatt Papier!

Read through a German newspaper article. Identify every example of a pronoun and write each one down, together with the noun it has replaced.

GLOSSAR

der Streit	argument
das Rätsel	puzzle
fehlen	to be missing
der Lippenstift	lipstick
der Bankangestellte	bank employee
der Hafen	harbour
das Segelboot	sailing boats
die Jacht	yacht
erledigen	to sort out, finish off

23

NEVER BY TRAIN TO BERLIN!
order of adverbs

 ## Auf die Plätze!

Order, order!

Whenever a German sentence contains elements which answer questions such as 'when did it happen?', 'how did they travel?', 'where is he sitting?', they should appear in a strict order.

1 Order of adverbs

These adverbial elements, which answer the questions *wann?*, *wie?* or *wo?*, should be placed in the sentence in the order: **Time – Manner – Place**

Am Montag	*bin ich*	***mit dem Zug***	***nach Mainz***	*gefahren.*
time/*wann?*		manner/*wie?*	place/*wo?*	

This procedure should be followed even if only two of the three elements described above occur:

Wir fahren	***nächstes Jahr***	***nach Japan***.
	time/*wann?*	place/*wo?*

 ## Toller Tipp!

It is very common for the time element to be placed at the very beginning of the sentence, as in the first example above. Even if other words come in between the three elements, the principle of **Time – Manner – Place** still operates. In fact, the rule is occasionally forgotten in spoken German, but it's important to try to remember it, especially when you are writing.

Fertig?

1 Wann – wie – wo?
Ordne diese Sätze!

Write these sentences in the right order.

1. mit dem Bus   Ich fahre   zur Schule   jeden Tag.
2. Mein Austauschpartner   aus Frankreich   gestern Abend   ist angekommen.
3. morgen   Hast du Lust,   zu gehen   zu einem   Fußballspiel?
4. vor dem Stadttheater   Steffi   ihren Freund   um sechs Uhr   treffen   soll.
5. Vater   bis acht Uhr   im Büro   arbeitet.
6. bleiben   gestern zu Hause   wegen schlechten Wetters   Wir mussten.

 ## Los!

2 Brief an Claudia
Schreibe einen Brief an deine Freundin, Claudia! Sag, was du letzte Woche gemacht hast!
Dein Terminkalender ist auf der nächsten Seite!

Write a letter to your friend Claudia. Tell her what you did last week; when, how and where. Your diary for the week is on the next page.

Beispiel:
> Am Montag habe ich im Stadtzentrum ein Buch und eine CD gekauft.

oder
> Am Montag bin ich mit dem Bus in die Stadt gefahren.

15 – Montag	Donnerstag – 18
Stadtzentrum (Bus) – Buch u. CD kaufen. Nicht vergessen – 18 Uhr – Tennis mit Lydia (Fahrrad).	Vormittag – Hausaufgaben (zu Hause). Abend – Kino m. Andreas (Bus)
16 – Dienstag	Freitag – 19
OMA BESUCHEN – BERLIN. Zug 10.30 Uhr.	14 Uhr Schwimmbad. m. Onkel Frank u. Ralf. (Onkel Franks Auto).
17 – Mittwoch	Samstag/Sonntag – 20/21
*Fahrradtour nach Potsdam.	WOCHENENDE –– Hurra! Samstag – Bootsfahrt mit Mutti/Vati. Sonntag, 9.30 Uhr – Gottesdienst

GLOSSAR

der Terminkalender   diary, appointments book

24

NO-ONE, NOTHING, NEVER!
negatives and word order

 Auf die Plätze!

Negatives

(*gar*) **nicht**	not (at all)	**nichts**	nothing
noch **nicht**	not yet	**kein**	not a(ny), no…
niemand	nobody	**keineswegs**	no way
nie(*mals*)	never	**null**	nil, nought, zero
nirgendwo	nowhere		

Rules, rules, rules! It's all a bit negative!
So far many of the rules of this language-game called German have been presented to you, but some games are more fun if you can work out the rules for yourself as you play along. The negative is a good opportunity for you to do so.

Study these negative sentences. Try to establish reliable rules affecting the postion of the negative in the sentence.

A
1. *Diese Musik gefällt mir (gar)* ***nicht!***
2. *Ich verstehe das* ***nicht!***
3. *Diese Musik finde ich* ***nicht*** *schön.*
4. *Spiel' mir diese Musik* ***nie*** *wieder!*
5. *Ich habe* ***keine*** *Ahnung!*
6. ***Keiner*** *hat es mir erklärt!*
7. ***Niemand*** *will mir helfen!*
8. *Kannst du mir* ***nicht*** *helfen?*

Grammatik Aktiv!

B
9a. *Das habe ich gar **nicht** verstanden!*
9b. *Das habe ich **nicht** total verstanden …*
10a. *Bist du **niemals** nach Amerika geflogen?*
10b. *Bist du nach Amerika **niemals** geflogen?*
11a. *Ich habe meine Hausaufgaben gestern **nicht** geschrieben!*
11b. *Ich habe meine Hausaufgaben **nicht** gestern geschrieben …*

You will hopefully have spotted some patterns:

1. Germans write '*kein-…*' instead of '*nicht ein-…*'.
2. A negative subject like '*niemand/keiner*' follows the same rules of word order as any subject.
3. The negative is often placed before the word which it particularly negates.
4. The negative is placed in different positions for emphasis.

Since a negative can refer to an **action (verb)**, a **description (adjective/ adverb)**, it is generally placed as close as possible to the word which it particularly negates. Compare:

a. *Wir fliegen heute **nicht**!*   We're **not** flying today!

Rules: 1. The verb *(fliegen)* must be the **second** element.
               2. The negative *(**nicht**)* at the **end** makes it **final**.

b *Wir fliegen **nicht** heute …*   We're **not** flying **today** …
   Here the negative applies to '***heute***':   i.e. **not today** but …

Practice makes perfect! Since negatives are often thus positioned for emphasis, practise **saying sentences aloud to yourself**, even without a partner. The more you practise, the sooner your ears will tell you if it **sounds right**.

 **Fertig?**

1 In Ordnung?
Ordne folgende Negativsätze!
Pass auf! Mehr als eine Lösung ist möglich!

Put the following negative sentences in the correct order.
Beware! More than one correct solution may be possible.

1. Nicht mir gefällt Rotwein.
2. Österreich warst niemals du in?
3. Geschwister ich keine habe.
4. Nichts wir zu verzollen haben.
5. Ihr Hausaufgaben keine habt gemacht?
6. Drogen mit niemals handelt!
7. Nichts gestern ich geschrieben habe!
8. Mein Geld ich kann finden nirgendwo.
9. Helfen keiner uns will?
10. Verstanden kein habe ich Wort!

H *2 Was passt wozu?*
Welche englische Übersetzung passt zu welchem deutschen Satz?

Match the English sentence to its German equivalent.

1. Ich bin nach Berlin niemals geflogen.
2. Ich bin niemals nach Berlin geflogen.
3. Das hat mir gar nicht geschmeckt.
4. Das hat mir nicht total geschmeckt.
5. Bonn besuchen wir morgen nicht.
6. Bonn besuchen wir nicht morgen.

a. We're not visiting Bonn **tomorrow** (but…)
b. I have never flown to **Berlin**.
c. **I really didn't** like the taste of that !
d. We're **not** visiting Bonn tomorrow !
e. I've never **flown** to Berlin (but…)
f. I didn't quite like the taste of that…

Los!

3 Die verneinte Form
Schreibe auf folgende Fragen mindestens eine verneinende Antwort!

Using the negatives listed above, write at least one negative answer to each of the following sentences.

Beispiel:

	A.	Wo hast du mein Geld gefunden?
	B. i.	Ich habe *kein* Geld gefunden!
bzw.	B. ii.	Dein Geld habe ich *nicht* gefunden!
bzw.	B. iii.	Ich habe dein Geld *nirgendwo* gefunden!
	usw.	

1. Hast du einen Bruder?
2. Wann haben Sie Salzburg besucht?
3. Wer kommt heute mit ins Kino?
4. Wohin seid ihr letztes Jahr auf Urlaub gefahren?
5. Wie hat dir das Eis geschmeckt?
6. Welche Mannschaft hat gewonnen?

4 Hotel Höllental!

Du hast furchtbare Ferien in einem deutschen Hotel verbracht. Schreibe einen Beschwerdebrief an den Hotelleiter, wo du alles beschreibst, was negativ war!

You are writing a letter of complaint to the manager of a German hotel, in which you have had a terrible holiday. Use as many different negatives as possible.

GLOSSAR

das stimmt doch nicht	that's just not true
keine Ahnung	no idea
erklären	to explain
verzollen	to declare taxable goods
geflogen	flown
handeln	to deal
verstanden	understood
Drogen	drugs

25

AND, BUT, ALTHOUGH, THAT
conjunctions

 **Auf die Plätze!**

What are conjunctions?
A clause is the basic unit in grammar, containing (usually) at least a subject, a verb and an object. Conjunctions are words which join two clauses.

> *Sandra ist fünfzehn Jahre alt **und** spielt viel Hockey.*
> Sandra is 15 years old **and** plays a lot of hockey.

1 Linking clauses with coordinating conjunctions

The commonest conjunctions in German are *und* (and), *aber* (but), *oder* (or), *denn* (for/because), *sondern* (but/in contrast). This group is known as 'coordinating conjunctions'.

> *Wir könnten draußen spielen **oder** möchtest du zu Hause bleiben?*
> We could play outside **or** would you like to stay in?

> *Thorsten ist nicht groß **sondern** (er ist) klein.*
> Thorsten is not big **but** small.

 Toller Tipp!

The subject does not need to be repeated in the second clause if it is the same as in the first, as in the example above.

2 Linking clauses with subordinate conjunctions

Another group of conjunctions behaves slightly differently. They send the verb in the subordinate clause (a secondary clause) to the end. You should always use a comma to separate a clause which begins with a subordinate conjunction.

*Peter war schon sehr müde, | | **als** ich ihn **traf**.*
Peter was already very tired when I met him.

The common subordinating conjunctions are:

als	when (past events)	*indem*	while
wenn	if, when(ever)	*ob*	whether
bevor	before	*seit*	since
bis	until	*während*	while, whereas
da	since	*weil*	because
dass	(the fact) that	*wie*	how
nachdem	after	*obwohl*	although
so dass	so that	*seitdem*	since then
als ob	as if		

*Er las das Buch, **bis** seine Schwester einschlief.*
He read the book, **until** his sister fell asleep.

*Steffi saß im Auto, **während** ich Milch kaufte.*
Steffi sat in the car **while** I bought milk.

*Ich weiß, **dass** ich hart arbeiten soll.*
I know **that** I should work hard.

 # Fertig?

1 Alles über Claudia
Claudia beschreibt alles, was zur Zeit bei ihr passiert. Verbinde die zwei Sätze mit der in Klammern angegebenen Konjunktion! Achte darauf, ob der Satzbau geändert werden muss!

Claudia is describing what's happening at the moment in her life. Link each pair of sentences with the conjunction in brackets. Be careful of changes in word order.

1. Mein Bruder Stefan isst gerne Erdbeeren. (aber) Ich esse lieber Himbeeren.
2. Jeden Tag übe ich Flöte. (bevor) Ich gehe zur Schule.
3. Unsere Lehrer sind böse auf uns. (weil) Wir haben unsere Hausaufgaben nicht gemacht.
4. Ich treffe meinen Freund. (wenn) Wir gehen in die Stadt.
5. Hast du gehört? (dass) Ich habe einen Kunstpreis gewonnen.

H *2 Alles über Kai*

Jetzt beschreibt Kai sein Leben. Diesmal fehlen sogar die Konjunktionen. Setze die passenden Konjunktionen aus dem Kasten ein, um die Lücken zu füllen!

Now Kai is describing his life. But this time even the conjunctions are missing. Put an appropriate conjunction, taken from the box, into the gap.

1. Ich gehe jeden Tag zu Fuß zur Schule, ... es oft regnet.
2. Ich liebe Filme .... gehe so oft wie möglich ins Kino.
3. Ich weiss, ... ich ein neues Fahrrad zum Geburtstag bekomme.
4. Meine Eltern sind immer böse auf mich, ... ich spät abends draußen bleibe.
5. Wir freuen uns, ... wir bald nach Eurodisney fahren.
6. Meine Klasse muss hart arbeiten, ... wir unseren Klassenausflug machen dürfen.

obwohl	wenn	weil	und	dass	bevor

Los!

H *3 Ende gut, alles gut*

Beende die untenstehenden Sätze! Verwende die vorgeschlagenen Bindewörter, um damit den nächsten Satzteil anzufangen!

Complete these two sentences, making use of the suggested conjunctions to begin the second clause.

1. Claudia trank meine Milch,   weil …
                                 bevor …
                                 aber ….

2. Max kaufte eine CD,   während …
                                 die …
                                 dass …

Beispiel:
Claudia trank meine Milch, weil sie großen Durst hatte.

GLOSSAR

einschlafen (sep)	to fall asleep
fleißig	hard working
Erdbeeren	strawberries
Himbeeren	raspberries
die Flöte	flute
der Kunstpreis	art prize
der Klassenausflug	class outing
sich freuen	to be pleased
böse	angry

26

THE MAN WHO ...
relative clauses

 **Auf die Plätze!**

What are relative clauses?

A relative clause, which follows a main clause, refers back to a noun in the main clause and offers extra information about it. Such a clause always begins with a **relative pronoun**.

> *Das ist die Brücke, **die** gestern in den Stürmen zusammenstürzte.*
> That's the bridge **which** collapsed in the storms yesterday.

1 Relative pronouns

Relative pronouns in German are almost exactly the same as the definite article forms, with one or two exceptions:

	Masculine	Feminine	Neuter	Plural
Nominative	*der*	*die*	*das*	*die*
Accusative	*den*	*die*	*das*	*die*
Genitive	***dessen***	***deren***	***dessen***	***deren***
Dative	*dem*	*der*	*dem*	***denen***

2 The relative pronoun in a relative clause

The relative pronoun must agree in gender and number with the noun or pronoun in the main clause, but does not necessarily agree in case.

Grammatik Aktiv!

■ If the person or thing in the relative clause is the **subject** of that clause, use a **nominative** pronoun – *der*, *das* or *die* (plural *die*):

> *Die Frau, __die dort sitzt__, ist hundert Jahre alt.*
>
> The woman **who is sitting there** is 100 years old.

> The woman is the subject of the relative clause, so *die* is nominative.

■ If the person or thing in the relative clause is the **object** of that clause, use an **accusative** pronoun – *den*, *das* or *die* (plural *die*):

> *Der Hund, __den wir fanden__, ist ein Schäferhund.*
>
> The dog **which we found** is an Alsatian.

> The dog is the object (we found it) so the relative pronoun has to be accusative.

■ If you are translating the English **possessive** pronoun 'whose', use a **genitive** pronoun – *dessen* or *deren* (plural *deren*):

> *Der Mann, __dessen Frau am Dienstag im Lotto gewann__, hat sich eine Jacht gekauft.*
> The man **whose** wife won the lottery on Tuesday has bought himself a yacht.

■ If you are using a **preposition**, or a **verb**, which requires a **dative (indirect) object**, in the relative clause, use a **dative** pronoun – *dem* or *der* (plural *denen*). Notice that in this case the relative clause does not necessarily begin with the relative pronoun:

> *Der Fotoapparat, __mit dem ich das Bild machte__, ist kaputt.*
> The camera, with which I took the picture, is broken.

■ *was* (which) can be used at the following times:

→ when *was* refers back to the demonstrative *das* (that):

> *Das, was sie nicht mehr mag.*
> the things she no longer likes.

➔ when it follows:

nichts	nothing
alles	everything
einiges	a few/some things
manches	a number of things
vieles	much/a lot of things
weniges	few things
etwas	something
folgendes	the following

Ich kaufe alles, was es gibt.
I'll buy everything that's there.

Er mochte manches, was in der Galerie war.
He liked a number of things in the gallery.

Du siehst vieles, was du nicht sehen solltest!
You see a lot of things you shouldn't see!

 Pass auf!

English has become quite lazy in this matter: some people now use 'that' as a relative pronoun, or leave the pronoun out altogether. Don't be tempted to use the German *dass*, or to say nothing.

*Der Computer, **den** ich will …*	The computer I want …
*Die Tasche, **die** ich fand, …*	The bag **that** I found …

3 Word order in relative clauses

A relative clause is always separated from the main clause by a comma, usually begins with a relative pronoun, and always has the verb at the end.

*Das ist der Mann, **der** meinen Fußball weggenommen hat.*
That's the man who took my football.

> Verb at the end

> The relative clause begins with a relative pronoun, which usually looks just like the definite article *der, die, das*. The form of the pronoun changes in the same way as the article, too.

> A comma separates the two clauses.

*Es ist ein Film, **der** ganz gut sein soll.*
It's a film which is meant to be very good.

Pass auf!

The German relative pronoun will reflect the gender and number of the person or thing being referred to, but may not agree with the case (nominative, accusative etc.) of the person or thing. Look at the above examples, which should make it clearer.

 # Fertig?

1 Lebensmittel vom Supermarkt
Setze die richtigen Relativpronomen vom untenstehenden Kasten ein!

Insert the correct relative pronouns from the box below.

1. Milch ist eine Flüssigkeit, … weiß ist und von Kühen kommt.
2. Gouda ist ein Käse, … ich sehr gerne esse.
3. Eine Orange ist eine Frucht, … Schale sehr bitter schmeckt.
4. Ich möchte vier Eiern, mit … ich einen Kuchen backen werde.
5. Fisch ist etwas, … ich nicht leiden kann.

denen	den	deren	das	die

2 Ein Ding, das …
Verbinde die zwei Sätze mit Relativpronomen!

Construct sentences using relative pronouns.

1. Ein Flugzeug ist eine Maschine.

Sie kann fliegen.

2. Herr Weichmantel ist ein Mann.

Er trägt einen Bart.

3. Ein Eisbär ist ein Tier.

Es hat ein weißes Fell.

4. Ich lese ein Buch.

Es ist sehr interessant.

5. Ein Porsche ist ein Wagen.

Er fährt sehr schnell.

6. Ein Wolkenkratzer ist ein Gebäude.

Es hat viele Stockwerke.

H *3 Ich kenne eine Person*
Fülle folgende Lücken mit dem treffenden Relativpronomen aus!

Fill in the gaps with the correct relative pronoun.

1. Ich kenne eine Frau, ... sechs Fremdsprachen kann.
2. Ich kenne einen Mann, ... Filmregisseur ist.
3. Ich kenne einen Lehrer, ... du auch kennst.
4. Ich kenne ein Mädchen, ... fünf Brüder hat.
5. Ich kenne ein Baby, ... rotes Haar hat.
6. Ich kenne den Jungen, mit ... du oft Fußball spielst.
7. Ich kenne eine Frau, ... Tochter Markus liebt.
8. Ich kenne die Lehrerin, mit ... meine Mutter spricht.
9. Ich kenne einen Mann, ... Haus zwei Million D-Mark kostet.
10. Ich kenne die Person, von ... Bernd sein Fahrrad gekauft hat.

Los!

⊞ 4 Wo ich wohne

Schreibe bzw. erzähle einem Freund oder einer Freundin, wie dein Haus und dein Zimmer aussehen! Verwende Relativpronomen, um mehr Information geben zu können.

Write down, or describe to a friend, what your house and bedroom are like. Use relative pronouns to allow you to add extra information.

Beispiel:

> Es ist ein Haus, das ziemlich groß ist.
> Ich habe eine CD-Anlage, die aus Japan kommt.

GLOSSAR

zusammenstürzen (sep.)	to collapse
der Sturm	storm
der Eisbär	polar bear
der Wolkenkratzer	skyscraper
die CD-Anlage	CD player
ziemlich	quite/relatively
aussehen	to look like
das Stockwerk	floor/storey
der Filmregisseur	film director
das Fell	fur
der Bart	beard
die Flüssigkeit	liquid
die Schale	peel/skin

27

FAST, FASTER, FASTEST
adjectives and adverbs

 **Auf die Plätze!**

What are adjectives and adverbs?
When we want to say what a thing is like – tall, interesting, long etc. – we use an
adjective. When we want to say how something is done – quickly, carefully etc. –
then we use an **adverb**. Both tend to be placed very close to the word which they
describe: adjectives to nouns, and adverbs to verbs.

1 Adjectives
If an adjective in German comes after the noun (and usually after *sein* or *werden*
too), you can use it without changes, exactly as you find it in a dictionary:

> *das Buch ist **rot***   *diese CD ist sehr **gut***   *mein Auto ist **schnell***

2 Adverbs
Similarly, if the adverb immediately follows its verb, the adverb is used in its
basic form:

> *er schreit **laut***   *sie tanzen **schön***   *er fährt sein Auto sehr **schnell***

 Pass auf!

Sometimes adverbs consist of more than just a single word. For example,
a preposition and a noun (and sometimes even an adjective as well) can be
used together as an adverb. This is called an **adverbial phrase**:

> *Ich wartete **mit Geduld**.*   I waited **with patience**.
>
> *Ich machte meine Arbeit*   I did my work without **any great**
> ***ohne große Probleme**.*   **problems**.

> *Ich lese das Buch mit dem* I am reading the book with the
> **größten*** *Interesse.* **greatest of interest.**
>
> NB*. If you use an adjective in the adverbial phrase, don't forget to add
> the correct ending (see Chapter 28).

Toller Tipp!

You might already have noticed that German adjectives and adverbs look
the same! *Schnell* can mean both 'quick', as in *das Auto ist schnell* and
'quickly', as in *Thomas läuft schnell*.

What are comparatives and superlatives?
You can use adjectives and adverbs when you want to compare two people or things
e.g. 'Lucy is old**er** than Stephen' or to pick one thing out of a group e.g. 'This is the
best book I have ever read'. This is called forming the comparative and superlative
of adjectives or adverbs.

3 Forming comparatives in German
Comparatives in German, like English, are formed by adding *-er* to the end of the
word.

schnell	→	*schneller*	quicker
schön	→	*schöner*	more beautiful/prettier

Dieter ist schneller als Sven. Dieter is faster than Sven.

Toller Tipp!

Notice the phrase '*schneller **als***', meaning 'faster **than**'. The German for
'**as** fast **as**' is '*so schnell **wie***'.

4 Forming superlatives in German
This time, remember to add *-(e)st* and the correct adjectival ending (see Chapter 28)
to the end of the basic word.

schnell	→	*der schnellste*	fastest
schön	→	*der schönste*	most beautiful/prettiest

If you want to use a superlative with a verb to say e.g. 'runs quickest' or 'shouts loudest' you should put *am* in front of it, and *-en* on the end of it.

*Joachim läuft **am** schnellsten.*	Joachim runs quickest.
*Richard spielt **am** schönsten Klavier.*	Richard plays the piano most beautifully.

 Pass auf!

Actually there are lots of times when you have to change the form of adjectives and adverbs in German. We will look at these cases in much more detail in the next chapter.

5 Irregular comparatives and superlatives

One important rule to note is that many adjectives and adverbs of just one syllable will add an umlaut to the vowel if possible:

groß	big	*größer*	*am größten*
alt	old	*älter*	*am ältesten*
jung	young	*jünger*	*am jüngsten*

And, as in English, there are some common forms which quite simply act rather strangely:

gut	good	*besser*	*am besten*
schlecht	bad	*schlimmer*	*am schlimmsten*
gern	gladly	*lieber*	*am liebsten*
viel	much	*mehr*	*am meisten*
hoch	high	*höher*	*am höchsten*

 Pass auf!

Some English adjectives use 'more' and 'most' to create their comparative and superlative forms. Don't be tempted to do the same with the German equivalents: mehr and meist.

Fertig?

1 Die Steigerungsformen
Schreibe nur die Komparativformen!

Fill in the comparative form only.

1.

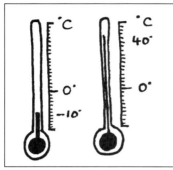

kalt – _____

2.

alt – _____

3.

schnell – _____

4.

teuer – _____

5.

klein – _____

6.

groß – _____

2 Die Steigerungsformen II
Fülle die Lücken aus!

Fill in the gaps.

SIMPLE	COMPARATIVE	SUPERLATIVE
groß	…	am größten
…	schöner	am schönsten
…	wichtiger	am wichtigsten
interessant	interessanter	am …
hoch	höher	am …
…	jünger	am …
…	…	am besten
früh	…	am …

H 3 Wer ist der Beste?
Vervollständige die Sätze!

Complete the sentences.

1. Jürgen läuft schnell. Stefan läuft … als Jürgen.
2. Alexandra spielt gut Klavier. Andreas spielt … als Alexandra.
3. Dieser Baum ist groß. Jener Baum … dieser.
4. Michas Katze ist sehr alt. Ankes Katze ist genau so … .
5. Heute ist es kalt. Gestern … .

4 Liebe Geschwister

Roland:

Ich bin 9 Jahre alt. Ich spiele ein bisschen Tennis. Ich bin 1,34 m groß. Ich spreche kein Englisch. Ich singe sehr gern.

Julia:

Ich bin 13 Jahre alt. Ich spiele sehr gut Tennis. Ich bin 1,80 m groß. Ich spreche gut Englisch. Ich höre gern Musik an.

Georg:

Ich bin 16 Jahre alt. Ich spiele Fußball. Ich bin 1,76 m groß. Ich spreche nicht so gut Englisch. Ich spiele gern Gitarre.

Julia, Roland und Georg sind Geschwister, die sich immer streiten. Sie vergleichen alles, was sie tun. Fülle den Kasten aus: wer ist größer, usw!

Julia, Roland and Georg are brothers and sisters who are always arguing. They compare everything that they do. Fill out the box below, saying who is bigger, etc.

	Julia	Roland	Georg
Alter:		ist der jüngste	1. _____
Tennis spielen:	2. _____		
Größe:	3. _____	4. _____	
Fremdsprachen:	5. _____		
Singen:		6. _____	

 Los!

5 Klassenumfrage

Frage in deiner Klasse herum! Wer singt schön, wer singt schöner? Wer ist der größte Schüler bzw. die größte Schülerin? Wer hat die längsten Haare? Schreibe die Ergebnisse auf!

Do a survey of your classmates. Who sings well, who sings better? Who is the tallest girl or boy? Who has the longest hair? Write down your results.

GLOSSAR

die Steigerungsformen	the comparative and superlative forms
fleißig	hard-working, conscientious
sich streiten	to argue with each other
vergleichen	to compare
die Umfrage	survey, census, questionnaire

28

SOME NEW TAPES
adjectival endings

 **Auf die Plätze!**

What is an adjective ending?
In the previous chapter we said that adjectives do not change if they are placed immediately after their noun, or in a sentence with *sein*. Otherwise, however, you have to change the ending of the adjective, depending on what exactly you are saying. The ending depends on the gender and case of the noun itself.

There are three groups of endings:

1 Group one endings
Definite article (the) + adjective + noun
If you have phrases using forms of *der*, *die*, *das* like '**the** rich woman', '**that** good book' or '**the** new film' use this group. You also use these endings for *dieser* (this), *jener* (that), *jeder* (each, every), *welcher?* (which?), *solcher* (such):

	Masculine	Feminine	Neuter	Plural
Nominative	*der neue Lehrer*	*die neue CD*	*das neue Auto*	*die neuen Bücher*
Accusative	*den neuen Lehrer*	*die neue CD*	*das neue Auto*	*die neuen Bücher*
Genitive	*des neuen Lehrers*	*der neuen CD*	*des neuen Autos*	*der neuen Bücher*
Dative	*dem neuen Lehrer*	*der neuen CD*	*dem neuen Auto*	*den neuen Büchern*

2 Group two endings
Indefinite article (a/an) + adjective + noun
If you have phrases using *ein*, *eine* etc. like '**an** old man', or '**my** favourite pet' use this group. You also use these endings for *kein* (no/none), and the possessives *mein* (my), *dein* (your), *ihr* (her), *sein* (his), *unser* (our), *euer* (your – plural), *Ihr* (your – polite), *ihr* (their) (for more on these words, see Chapter 6):

	Masculine	Feminine	Neuter	Plural
Nominative	*ein alter Mann*	*eine reiche Dame*	*ein gutes Buch*	*die großen Bäume*
Accusative	*einen alten Mann*	*eine reiche Dame*	*ein gutes Buch*	*die großen Bäume*
Genitive	*eines alten Mannes*	*einer reichen Dame*	*eines guten Buchs*	*der großen Bäume*
Dative	*einem alten Mann*	*einer reichen Dame*	*einem guten Buch*	*den großen Bäumen*

3 Group three endings
adjective + noun alone
If you have phrases like 'good food', 'German beer' or 'fresh milk' follow this pattern:

	Masculine	Feminine	Neuter	Plural
Nominative	*guter Wein*	*schöne Musik*	*deutsches Bier*	*schnelle Autos*
Accusative	*guten Wein*	*schöne Musik*	*deutsches Bier*	*schnelle Autos*
Genitive	*guten Weins*	*schöner Musik*	*deutschen Biers*	*schneller Autos*
Dative	*gutem Wein*	*schöner Musik*	*deutschem Bier*	*schnellen Autos*

■ Following *etwas* (something), *nichts* (nothing), *viel* (much) and *wenig* (little), the adjective begins with a capital letter and follows the Group 3, neuter singular endings:

Nominative	*viel Gutes*	many good things
Accusative	*viel Gutes*	
Genitive	*viel Guten*	
Dative	*viel Gutem*	

■ After *einige* (some, a few), *folgende* (following), *manche* (some), *mehrere* (several), *viele* (many) and *wenige* (few) the adjective takes Group Three plural endings. eg: *manche interessante Bücher* (some interesting books), *mit einigen netten Leuten* (with some nice people).

■ Do not decline *viel* and *wenig* when they are used as adverbs or come before singular uncountable nouns, eg: *viel süßer Orangensaft* (a lot of sweet orange juice); *ich laufe wenig* (I walk very little).

Pass auf!

Adjectives following *alles* behave like this:

Nominative	*alles Neue*
Accusative	*alles Neue*
Genitive	*alles Neuen*
Dative	*alles Neuem*

 Toller Tipp!

Don't worry if it all seems very complicated at first: it takes a long time to get used to all the different endings here! As you learn them, though, see if you can find a pattern which helps you. Notice how the Group 1 endings are quite straightforward, because a lot of the information about the noun's gender and case is revealed by the article. As you work through the Group 2 and Group 3 endings, there is less and less information in the article, and there is none at all in Group 3. So the adjectival ending starts looking more and more like the endings you learned for the definite article.

> *Der Wein ist gut* ➔ *Er ist guter Wein*
> *Ich trinke den Wein* ➔ *Ich trinke deutschen Wein*

It doesn't work for every single ending, but it should help to get you started!

 **Fertig?**

1 Ganz im Gegenteil
Schreibe diese Sätze mit einem gegensätzlichen Adjektiv!

Change the adjective in the sentence to turn the meaning into the opposite.

1. Das war ein sehr interessantes Buch. (langweilig)
2. Kennst du meinen älteren Bruder? (jünger)
3. Er hat viel guten Wein getrunken. (schlecht)
4. Ich möchte einen schwarzen Regenschirm kaufen. (weiß)
5. Was macht ihr mit euren alten Platten? (neu)
6. Ich mag langsame Autos sehr. (schnell)

2 Weihnachtswünsche
Was wünschen sich Freddie und Tina zu Weihnachten?

What do Freddie and Tina want for Christmas?

Grammatik Aktiv!

Beispiel:

Freddie wünscht sich ein schnelles Fahrrad.

Freddie wünscht sich:

1. ein Fahrrad

schnell

2. einen Fußball

gut

3. einen Computer

toll

4. ein Paar Schuhe

schwarz

Tina wünscht sich:

5. eine Stereo-Anlage

modern

6. einen Papagei

bunt

7. ein Hemd

blau

8. eine Jeans-Hose

neu

3 Was ich zur Zeit lese

Thomas hat einen Aufsatz geschrieben. Der Titel hieß 'Was ich zur Zeit lese.' Dafür hat er aber die Note 'mangelhaft' bekommen. Er muss den Aufsatz neu schreiben, und zwar mit mehr Adjektiven. Hilf dem Thomas dabei: Du musst die richtigen Adjektive auswählen und sie dann richtig in die Lücken einfügen.

Thomas has written an essay entitled 'What I'm reading at the moment'. But he got a bad mark for it. He has to rewrite the essay adding some adjectives. Help Thomas to rewrite it: choose the appropriate adjective for each gap and insert it with the correct ending.

Letzte Woche las ich ein ganz … Buch. Es war ein … Roman. Der … Held und seine … Partnerin fuhren nach Deutschland. Sie mussten eine … Mission durchführen. Sie flogen nach Berlin in einem … Flugzeug. Dort haben sie einen … Agenten kennengelernt, der ihnen … Pläne verkauft hatte. Sie brachten die … Pläne zum Hauptquartier des … Geheimdiensts zurück. Am Ende dieser … Geschichte hat sich der Held in seine … Partnerin verliebt, was mir gar nicht gefiel!

gefährlich	interessant	jung	groß	fremd	jung	britisch
spannend	hübsch	teuer	großartig	wichtig		

Los!

⊞ 4 Zoobesuch

Du hast mit Freunden den Zoo besucht. Beschreibe ein Tier – ohne seinen Namen zu verraten – bis jemand es errät!

You and your friends have just been to the zoo. Describe one of the animals – without saying its name – until somebody guesses which one it is.

Beispiel:

Beschreibung: Dieses Tier ist sehr groß. Es hat sehr lange Beine und kann die grünen Blätter in den Bäumen essen. Auf seiner gelben Haut gibt es braune Flecken.

Antwort: Giraffe

Ein paar Vorschläge:	Löwe	Bär	Pinguin	Adler	Eisbär	Elefant

H *5 Regenbogenspiel*
Beschreibe Gegenstände, Kleidungsstücke oder Personen im Klassenzimmer bzw. zu Hause mit allen möglichen Farben!
Die Farben im Regenbogen sind:

rot   orange   gelb   grün   blau   indigo   violett

Vergiss auch nicht: hell- und dunkel-, Streifen, Punkte, Karos usw!

Describe objects, clothing and people in your classroom or at home, using all the colours you can imagine. The colours of the rainbow are:

red   orange   yellow   green   blue   indigo   violet

Don't forget: light and dark, stripes, dots, checks etc!

Beispiel:
> Unser Lehrer trägt eine rote Krawatte.

GLOSSAR

der Papagei	parrot
bunt	colourful
der Aufsatz	essay
die Note	mark, grade
mangelhaft	'lacking', not very good
vorschlagen	to suggest
spannend	exciting
der Roman	novel
gefährlich	dangerous
fremd	strange, unknown
das Hauptquartier	headquarters
der Geheimdienst	secret service
großartig	terrific
sich in jemanden verlieben	to fall in love with somebody
der Gegenstand	object
Streifen	stripes
Punkte	dots, spots
Karos	squares, diamonds

29

WHEN I WAS YOUNG, I HAD ...
the imperfect tense

Auf die Plätze!

What is the imperfect?
The imperfect is a tense used to describe events that happened in the past.
Generally, it is used only in more formal German nowadays, especially when
writing. To be able to read a German-language newspaper, for instance, you will
need to know the imperfect forms of common verbs. In spoken German only a
limited number of verbs are used regularly in the imperfect tense.

1 Formation
There are three different groups of imperfect forms of verbs, and you need to know
to which group a particular verb belongs: **weak**, **strong** or **mixed**.

a Weak verbs
To form the imperfect of a weak verb take the stem and add the following endings:
-te, -test, -te, -ten, -tet, -ten

wohnen – to live (in)   stem: *wohn-*

ich wohnte	I lived	*wir wohnten*	we lived
du wohntest	you lived	*ihr wohntet*	you lived
er/sie/es wohnte	he lived	*sie/Sie wohnten*	they/you lived

b Strong verbs
These verbs use a modified stem, plus the following endings: (-), *-st*, (-), *-en*, *-t*, *-en*

singen – to sing   stem: *sang-*

ich sang	I sang	*wir sangen*	we sang
du sangst	you sang	*ihr sangt*	you sang
er/sie/es sang	he sang	*sie/Sie sangen*	they/you sang

c Mixed verbs

A small group of verbs both modify their stem and follow the pattern of weak endings:

denken – to think   stem: *dach-*

ich dachte	I thought	*wir dachten*	we thought
du dachtest	you thought	*ihr dachtet*	you thought
er/sie/es dachte	he thought	*sie/Sie dachten*	they/you thought

2 Common imperfect verbs

Nowadays it is considered acceptable to use the perfect tense for a lot of everyday German referring to the past. There are just a few verbs, however, which are almost always used in the imperfect. You should familiarise yourself with them as quickly as you can, and use them in your own German phrases when referring to the past.

sein – to be

ich war	*wir waren*
du warst	*ihr wart*
er/sie/es war	*sie/Sie waren*

haben – to have

ich hatte	*wir hatten*
du hattest	*ihr hattet*
er/sie/es hatte	*sie/Sie hatten*

 Pass auf!

The imperfect of *sein* and *haben* can act as auxiliaries when forming the pluperfect tense. For more information on this, see Chapter 32.

The modal verbs, too, are often used in the imperfect, especially:

	können	*müssen*	*sollen*	*wollen*	*dürfen*
	was able to	had to	was supposed to	wanted to	was allowed to
ich	*konnte*	*musste*	*sollte*	*wollte*	*durfte*
du	*konntest*	*musstest*	*solltest*	*wolltest*	*durftest*
er/sie/es	*konnte*	*musste*	*sollte*	*wollte*	*durfte*
wir	*konnten*	*mussten*	*sollten*	*wollten*	*durften*
ihr	*konntet*	*musstet*	*solltet*	*wolltet*	*durftet*
sie/Sie	*konnten*	*mussten*	*sollten*	*wollten*	*durften*

Ich war letztes Jahr in Frankfurt.	I was in Frankfurt last year.
Für meine Arbeit bekam ich eine Eins!	I got a 1 for my homework!
Ich musste am Wochenende mein Zimmer aufräumen.	I had to tidy my room at the weekend
Ich wollte dir sagen, dass …	I wanted to tell you that …

Toller Tipp!

You will find the verb tables for all the different tenses and categories of verb laid out in full at the back of this book. See Chapter 36, Appendix I.

Fertig?

H *1 Erinnerungen an die Sommerferien*
Gerlindes Oma beschreibt ihre Schulferien aus der Zeit, als sie noch Kind war. Setze alle Verbformen aus dem Präsens ins Präteritum!

Gerlinde's grandma is describing her school holidays when she was a child. Turn all present tense verbs into the imperfect.

Das **ist** im Jahre 1928. In den Schulferien **besuche** ich meine Oma in Lahnstein am Rhein. Es **ist** sehr schön, weil meine Oma in einem großen Haus **wohnt**. Sie **hat** ein paar Hühner und jeden Tag **gehe** ich auf den Hof, um sie zu füttern.

Omas Nachbar **heißt** Herr Reuter. Er **hat** ein Motorrad und manchmal **nimmt** er mich mit, wenn er nach Köln **fährt**. Dann **sehe** ich den Kölner Dom und **darf** all die schönen Läden besuchen. Danach **essen** wir immer ein Eis, bevor wir nach Lahnstein **zurückkehren**.

Ich **schlafe** nachts in einem Zimmer hoch im Hausdach. Ich **habe** immer ein bisschen Angst, weil ich zu Hause mein Schlafzimmer mit meinem Bruder **teile**.

Meine Oma **lebt** alleine in dem Haus – mein Opa **stirbt** schon im ersten Weltkrieg – aber sie **ist** nie einsam. Wir **haben** eine sehr schöne Zeit miteinander und ich **freue** mich jedes Jahr, wenn ich wieder zu ihr **fahre**.

Grammatik Aktiv!

2 Im Polizeirevier

Kommissar Klempner hat ein Gespräch mit Claudia Kralle, einer Einbrecherin. Du bist sein(e) Assistent(in). Schreibe alles im Präteritum auf, was Frau Kralle sagt! Welche Aussage stimmt?

You are taking notes for Kommissar Klempner while he interviews Claudia Kralle, a burglar. Using the imperfect, write down what she says. Which of her statements is likely to be true?

Beispiel:

    Klempner: Was haben Sie am Wochenende gemacht?
    Kralle: Ich bin ins Kino gegangen.

    Du schreibst: *Sie ging ins Kino.*

1. Ich habe meine Schwester in Berlin besucht.
2. Mein Freund und ich sind in Österreich Ski gefahren.
3. Ich bin ganz faul gewesen – ich habe nichts gemacht!
4. Ich habe das ganze Wochenende lang geschlafen!
5. Freunde haben mit mir meinen Geburtstag gefeiert.
6. Ich habe ferngesehen.
7. Ich bin in ein großes Haus eingebrochen.

3 Was stimmt: 1, 2 oder 3?
Wähl die richtige Übersetzung!

Choose the correct translation.

1. er musste   she wanted / he had to / he mixed
2. wir schliefen   we slipped / we slept / we sang
3. du kamst   you listened / they saw / you came
4. Sie saßen   you sat / you went / you called
5. ich las   I lay / I read / she bought
6. they listened   sie hörten / sie schliefen / sie hören
7. I wanted   es ging / ich folgte / ich wollte
8. we asked   wir fragten / wir bitten / er nahm
9. you saw (polite)   du siehst / Sie sahen / ihr solltet
10. he played   er spielt / er spielte / er schrieb

4 Wann passierte das?
Fülle die Lücken, mit Hilfe eines Verbs im Präteritum, aus!

Fill in the gaps with a verb in the imperfect.

1. 1492 ... Columbus Amerika.
2. 1789 ... die französische Revolution.
3. 1901 ... Königin Viktoria von England.
4. 1918 ... der erste Weltkrieg.
5. 1969 ... Neil Armstrong auf dem Mond.
6. 1991 ... die Deutschen die Wiedervereinigung.

feiern	beginnen	sterben	landen	entdecken	enden

Los!

⊞ 5 Kurz gefasst
Suche einen interessanten Artikel in einer deutschsprachigen Zeitung! Schreibe dann eine Zusammenfassung des Artikels! Verwende wenn möglich, das Imperfekt!

Find an interesting article in a German newspaper. Then write a summary of the article in German, using imperfect forms of the verbs wherever possible.

⊞ 6 Perfektes Tennis
Spiel Perfektes Tennis mit einem Freund/einer Freundin am Tisch! Sag einen Satz mit einem Verb im Perfekt (z.B. 'ich habe meine Hausaufgaben gemacht'). Wenn dein Gegner innerhalb von 5 Sekunden den Satz nicht ins Präteritum umsetzen kann (d.h. 'ich machte meine Hausaufgaben'), dann bekommst du einen Punkt; wenn doch, dann bekommt er/sie den Punkt. Wenn du einen Punkt gewinnst, darfst du den nächsten Satz sagen.

Play a game of 'perfect – imperfect tennis' with a partner. Throw a 'serve' by calling out a sentence with the verb in the perfect tense. Give your partner 5 seconds to answer with the correct imperfect version. If s/he answers correctly, s/he receives a point, otherwise the point goes to you. If you win the point, you start again.

GLOSSAR

das Huhn	chicken
füttern	to feed (animals)
zurückkehren	to return
sterben	to die
einsam	lonely
einziehen	to move into (house)
faul	lazy
spazieren gehen	to go for a walk
das Ereignis	event
entdecken	to discover
feiern	to celebrate
die Wiedervereinigung	reunification
einbrechen (sep.)	to break in
die Zusammenfassung	summary

30

A BOY HAS BEEN ATTACKED
the passive voice

 **Auf die Plätze!**

What is the passive?

Normally a sentence containing the three basic elements – **subject**, **verb form**, and **object** – tells us that somebody does something.

John schreibt einen Brief.   John is writing a letter.

But **sometimes this order is turned around**, to say that the thing **was done by** somebody.

Der Brief wurde von John geschrieben.   The letter was written by John.

This is called the **passive voice**. It makes the object of a normal sentence the subject instead.

1 Formation
The passive voice is particularly common in newspaper reports. Look at the following examples, before we discuss the formation of the passive in detail. Despite some new vocab, you should be able to read the stories without any problems, even though you probably have not studied the passive before.

DIE NACHRICHTEN AUF EINEM BLICK

Neuer Präsident

Am Montag wird ein neuer Bundespräsident gewählt. Man glaubt, dass zum erstenmal eine Präsidentin das Amt bekleiden wird.

Flugzeug abgeschossen

Heute früh ist ein amerikanisches Kampfflugzeug abgeschossen worden. Der Pilot konnte sich durch seinen Schleudersitz retten und wurde per Hubschrauber zurück zu seinem Flugzeugträger „Nimitz" in Sicherheit gebracht.

Junge wurde angegriffen

Gestern Nacht wurde ein fünfzehnjähriger Junge im Stadtzentrum angegriffen. Dabei wurde er glücklicherweise nicht schwer verletzt. Die Täter – etwa vier bis sechs Jugendliche – werden noch immer von der Polizei gesucht.

You might have been able to work out that the passive is usually formed with a part of the verb **werden** plus a **past participle** (see Chapter 19 for more information about the past participle). We'll look at the passive voice forms in the newspaper articles now, comparing them with the active voice equivalents.

a Present/Future

*Das Volk **wählt** am Montag einen neuen Präsidenten.*

The people will **elect** a new president on Monday.

*Ein neuer Präsident **wird** am Montag vom Volk **gewählt.***

A new president will be **elected** by the people on Monday.

b Imperfect

*Punks **griffen** einen 15-jährigen Jungen **an**.*

Punks **attacked** a 15-year old boy.

*Ein 15-jähriger Junge **wurde** von Punks **angegriffen**.*

A 15-year old boy **was attacked** by punks.

c Perfect

*Der Feind **hat** ein Flugzeug **abgeschossen**.*

The enemy **has shot down** a plane.

*Ein Flugzeug **ist** vom Feind **abgeschossen worden**.*

A plane **has been shot down** by the enemy.

As you look at each sentence, bear the following points in mind:

- The passive is formed by a form of *werden* + past participle.

- The tense of *werden* stays the same as that of the main verb in the equivalent, active sentence.

- In each sentence, the object of the active sentence is now the subject of the passive voice. In German, this causes a change in case (accusative to nominative).

- The new subject dictates whether the verb should be singular or plural.

- The main verb of the active sentence is now a past participle form, placed at the end of the clause.

 Pass auf!

You will have seen *werden* being used to form a tense, the future, earlier on. Don't get the different uses of *werden* mixed up – refer back to Chapter 18 for revision of the future tense if you are not sure. Remember too, that *werden* has the basic meaning 'to become'.

2 The impersonal pronoun *'man'*

Although the English impersonal pronoun 'one' is hardly used any more, the German *man* is much more common and a useful alternative to using the passive.

Ein neuer Präsident wird gewählt. ➔ *Man wird einen neuen Präsidenten wählen.*

Ein Dieb wurde verhaftet. ➔ *Man hat einen Dieb verhaftet.*

 Toller Tipp!

Another way of avoiding the use of a particular subject (ich, du, er, sie, etc.) is to use the impersonal constructions *es gibt* ..., *es geht* ..., *es tut* ..., e.g.,

Es gibt vier hundert in der Gruppe.
There are four hundred in the group.

Es geht leider nicht.
Sorry, that doesn't work. OR
Sorry, that's impossible.

Es tut wirklich gut!
It really does you good!

Fertig?

1 Schlagzeilen

Verwende die richtige Form von 'werden', um die Schlagzeilen zu vervollständigen!

Complete the newspaper headlines with the correct form of 'werden'.

1. Nach dem Bootsunglück   …   noch 4 Personen vermisst.
    After the boat accident 4 people are still missing.

2. Die Regierung   …   für die neueste Wirtschaftskrise verantwortlich gemacht.
    The government is being blamed for the latest economic crisis.

3. Aus der Hauptstadt   …   heftige Gefechte berichtet.
    Serious fights were reported in the capital city.

4. Nach dem Autounfall   …   drei Personen ins Krankenhaus eingeliefert.
    After the car accident 3 people have been taken to hospital.

5. Die Reform der deutschen Sprache   …   innerhalb von fünf Jahren eingeleitet.
    The reform of the German language will be introduced within 5 years.

H 2 Die Verwandlung

Folgende Sätze sind alle im Aktiv geschrieben worden. Schreibe sie im Passiv neu!

Rewrite the following, active sentences in the passive voice.

1. Die Polizei hat am Dienstag einen berüchtigten Dieb verhaftet.
    Ein berüchtigter Dieb … .

2. Man verlieh letzten Dienstag die Oscars für dieses Jahr.
    Die Oscars … .

3. Schreibt bitte diese Arbeit mit größter Sorgfältigkeit!
    Die Arbeit … .

4. Freitags isst man immer Fisch.
    Fisch … .

5. Das Berliner Stadtorchester hat sein nächstes Konzert abgesagt.
    Das nächste Konzert … .

Los!

3 Zeitungslektüre

Suche Beispiele für das Passiv in einer deutschsprachigen Zeitung! Schreibe die Beispiele auf!

Look for examples of the passive voice in a German newspaper. Write out the examples.

4 Und jetzt, die Nachrichten

Mit den Sätzen, die in Übung 3 gefunden wurden, schreibe den Text für die aktuellen Nachrichten! Nimm die Nachrichten auf Kassette (Radionachrichten) oder sogar auf Video (Fernsehnachrichten) auf!

Use the sentences from Exercise 3 to write a script for a news programme. Record them onto tape, for a radio news programme, or on video to make a TV news broadcast.

GLOSSAR

ein Amt bekleiden	to take up office
angreifen (sep.)	to attack
der Täter	perpetrator, culprit
das Kampfflugzeug	fighter aircraft
abschießen	to shoot down
der Schleudersitz	ejector seat
der Flugzeugträger	aircraft carrier
treffen	(here) to kick
verhaften	to arrest
die Schlagzeile	headline

31

'IF I WERE YOU, I WOULD ...'
conditional and subjunctive

 **Auf die Plätze!**

What is the conditional?

Believe it or not, you will already be familiar with a number of German phrases using conditional or subjunctive forms of verbs, e.g. *ich möchte, ich hätte gern, könntest du?* etc. Other forms are becoming increasingly rare. Nevertheless, the conditional and the subjunctive play various roles in German that you should at least be aware of.

The conditional, frequently used with the conjunction *wenn* in German, links two possible events, where one must happen before the other can take place.

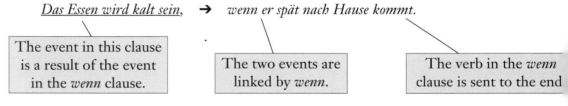

Das Essen wird kalt sein, ➔ *wenn er spät nach Hause kommt.*

The event in this clause is a result of the event in the *wenn* clause.

The two events are linked by *wenn*.

The verb in the *wenn* clause is sent to the end

The food will be cold if he arrives home late.

1 Conditional sentences

In its simplest form, a conditional sentence using *wenn*, links two concrete statements. Being a subordinate conjunction (see Chapter 25 for more information about these), *wenn* sends the verb to the end of the clause.

Ich werde nicht im Garten arbeiten können, wenn es regnet.
I won't be able to work in the garden if it rains.

In fact, the order of the two clauses can be reversed, but notice one important change to the word order within the clauses if you do this.

*Wenn es regnet, **werde ich** nicht im Garten arbeiten können.*

However, if the condition being talked about is more abstract, or if there is an element of doubt about one of the events, a German speaker might use the **subjunctive**.

What is the subjunctive?
The subjunctive has all but disappeared in English. A well-known song goes 'If I were a rich man…' and we sometimes say 'If I were you, I would …'. Both of these sentences imply a sense of disbelief, or that the event is unlikely. This is the subjunctive.

2 Common subjunctive forms
In German, too, the subjunctive is becoming less common, but it is used more than in English. Look at these forms:

	sein		haben	werden	mögen
ich	sei	wäre	hätte	würde	möchte
du	sei(e)st	wärst	hättest	würdest	möchtest
er/sie/es	sei	wäre	hätte	würde	möchte
wir	seien	wären	hätten	würden	möchten
ihr	seiet	wäret	hättet	würdet	möchtet
sie/Sie	seien	wären	hätten	würden	möchten

In fact, many of these forms are hardly ever used nowadays. Here are some of the commonest phrases which use a subjunctive in German.

*Wenn ich an deiner Stelle **wäre**, **würde** ich …* — If I **were** you, I **would** …
*Ich **hätte gerne** eine Cola, bitte.* — I'd **like** a cola, please.
*Ich **möchte** zwei Briefmarken zu 1,-DM.* — I'd **like** two DM 1 stamps, please.
*Wir fahren bald, **es sei denn**, der Martin kommt spät.* — We'll get off soon, **unless** Martin's late.

3 The subjunctive used to report speech
In German the subjunctive is used to report speech. The tense of the original statement is kept, but the verb is put into the subjunctive form. Again, this is also becoming less common in spoken German, but it is still very common in written German, especially in the press. (Note how English, in contrast, changes the tense in these examples.)

Der Politiker sagte: 'Mein Gegner ist ein Lügner'.
= *Der Politiker sagte, sein Gegner **sei** ein Lügner.*
The politician said that his opponent **was** a liar.

Ein Sprecher der Polizei sagte: 'Der Fahrer hat einen Unfall gebaut'.
= *Nach einem Sprecher der Polizei **habe** der Fahrer einen Unfall gebaut.*
According to a police spokesman the driver **had** caused an accident.

Der alte Mann sagte an seinem 100. Geburtstag: 'Harte Arbeit kann niemandem schaden.'
= *An seinem 100. Geburtstag sagte Herr Genscher, harte Arbeit **könne** niemandem schaden.*
On his 100th birthday Herr Genscher said that hard work **could** not harm anyone.

Don't panic, therefore, if you see a strange verb form like this, often (though not always) with an umlaut modification that you have not seen before. If it is in a passage where a person, a spokesman or a report is being quoted, then translate it using English reported speech.

4 Perfect subjunctive of modals

To say 'should have done', or 'could have stayed' etc., use one of the modal verbs plus the normal auxiliary in a subjunctive form. It is probably one of the hardest constructions you'll ever come across in German, but this is only an introduction, so study these examples and see if you can spot the pattern.

*Du **hättest** mir **sagen können**, dass du Fisch nicht magst!*
You **could have told** me that you don't like fish!

*Ihr **hättet wissen sollen**, dass man im Klassenzimmer nicht Fußball spielen darf.*
You **should have known** that you aren't allowed to play football in the classroom.

So a **subjunctive auxiliary (*hätte* etc.) + verb + modal past participle** gives the equivalent to the English 'should have done', 'ought to have said', 'could have helped', where an event might have taken place, but in fact didn't.

Note: with modal verbs, the infinitive acts as the past participle (i.e. *sollen* rather than *gesollt*).

 Toller Tipp!

You will find all the appropriate verb forms in Chapter 36, Appendix I.

 **Fertig?**

🅷 *1 Wenn es nur so leicht wäre!*
Finde die Sätze, die zueinander passen!

Put together the appropriate halves to make complete sentences.

1. Wenn ich an deiner Stelle wäre,
2. Ich werde mich sehr freuen,
3. Wenn ich nach Deutschland fahre,
4. Was willst du machen,
5. BMW wird eine neue Fabrik eröffnen,
6. Wenn ich im Lotto gewinnen würde,
7. Möchten Sie Kinder haben,
8. Wenn ich dir 20,-DM gäbe,

   a. wenn du Geburtstag hast?
   b. würde ich einen Urlaub in Australien machen.
   c. wenn Sie heiraten?
   d. wenn ich einen Computer zum Geburtstag bekomme.
   e. würde ich das nicht tun!
   f. wenn es den Vertrag bekommt.
   g. würdest du meinen Aufsatz schreiben?
   h. schicke ich dir eine Postkarte.

🅷 *2 Kurz und bündig*
Lies die 3 Geschichten, die aus der Zeitung ausgeschnitten worden sind! Fülle die Lücken mit den Konjunktivformen auf der nächsten Seite aus!

The 3 newspaper stories below have had all the subjunctive forms cut out. Read the stories and fill in the gaps with the conjunctive forms given on the next page.

Nie mehr Fenster putzen?

Nach Angaben des Saarbrückener Instituts für Neue Materialien … es jetzt möglich, nie mehr die Fenster putzen zu müssen. Es … sich um eine schmutzabweisende und kratzfeste transparente Antihaftbeschichtung, die sich chemisch mit dem Grundmaterial …

Bericht aus dem Parlament.

Gestern ist der Bundeskanzler stark angegriffen worden. Laut Oppositions-mitgliedern … er neulich mit seiner Sekretärin zwei Tage lang nach Schweden gefahren. Ein MdB hat gesagt, er … eine eindeutige Erklärung dafür, da er … es … um ein Sexskandal. Der Bundeskanzler antwortete darauf, er und seine Sekretärin … dorthin geflogen, um ein Geschenk für seine Frau zu kaufen. Die Reise … ganz unschuldig, behauptete er.

Tragischer Zwischenfall

Ein 32-Jahre alter Tourist … gestern von einem Unbekannten in einem Hotel in Thailand getötet worden, hieß es im Bonner Auslandsamt. Die beiden Männer … sich gestritten, wobei der Deutsche dann erstochen worden … . Der Täter, hieß es im Polizeibericht, … geflohen, bevor man ihn verhaften … . Der Tourist starb drei Stunden später im Krankenhaus.

könnte	sei	wolle	verbinde	handele	sei	seien
sei	vermute	gehe	sei	hätten	wäre	sei

 Los!

H 3 Journalistenauftrag I

Finde in einer deutschsprachigen Zeitung Beispiele für die indirekte Rede, Konjunktivformen und Konditionalsätzen! Schreibe dann einen Text und mache deine eigene Nachrichtensendung!

Find examples of reported speech, subjunctives and conditional sentences in a German-language newspaper. Copy them out and produce your own news bulletin.

H 4 Journalistenauftrag II

Jetzt schreibe Artikel über aktuelle Ereignisse in deiner Klasse, Schule oder Stadt!

Now write your own news items about what's going on in your own class, school or town. Interview friends (in German) about these events, then report them using subjunctive verbs, where possible.

GLOSSAR

der Gegner	opponent
der Lügner	liar
schaden	to hurt, harm
die Fabrik	factory
der Vertrag	contract
nach Angaben (von)	... according to ...
schmutzabweisend	dirt repelling
die Antihaftbeschichtung	non-stick layer
verbinden	to bind, stick
eindeutig	clear
vermuten	to suspect
behaupten	to claim
das Auslandsamt	Foreign Office
MdB (Mitglied des Bundestags)	MP
erstechen	to stab

32

WHEN I HAD LEFT ...
pluperfect tense

 Auf die Plätze!

What is the pluperfect?
The pluperfect tells us about what **had** happened in the past, probably quite a while ago.

*Es **hat** über Nacht geregnet.*	It has rained overnight. (perfect – recently in the past)
*Es **regnete**, als sie heirateten.*	It rained/was raining when they got married. (imperfect – longer ago)
*Es **hatte** vierzig Tage lang geregnet.*	It had rained for forty days. (pluperfect – even longer ago)

In fact, the pluperfect is not a tense that you will use very often in GCSE, but is useful nevertheless. At the very least, you should learn to recognise it when you come across it.

1 Formation of the pluperfect
The pluperfect is very **similar to the perfect tense** (see Chapter 19), but it describes an event which happened **further in the past**, usually longer ago than something in the other past tenses. Look at these examples:

Perfect	**Pluperfect**
Suzanne hat die Tür geschlossen.	*Stefan **hatte** das Fenster geschlossen.*
Suzanne (has) closed the door.	Stefan **had** closed the window.
Wir haben Oma besucht.	*Wir **hatten** Onkel Peter besucht.*
We (have) visited grandma.	We **had** visited uncle Peter.

Ich bin nach Kanada gefahren.
I (have) travelled to Canada.

*Ich **war** nach Neuseeland gefahren.*
I **had** travelled to New Zealand.

In each case, the only difference is that the auxiliary – whether *sein* or *haben* – is now in the imperfect. The past participle of the verb is exactly the same in both tenses.

Toller Tipp!

A few phrases to help you talk about events in the past.

■ **How long has it been happening?**

*Ich lerne Deutsch **seit** vier Jahren.*
I have been learning German **for** four years.

■ **How long had it been happening?**

*Ich lernte Deutsch **seit** vier Jahren.*
I had been learning German **for** four years.

■ **How long did something last?**

*Ich war drei Wochen **lang** in Deutschland.*
I was in Germany **for** three weeks.

■ **How long ago did something happen?**

*Ich war **vor** sechs Jahren in Amerika.*
I was in America six years **ago**.

■ **Something that had just happened, when …**

*Ich hatte die Polizei gerade angerufen, **als** es klingelte.*
I had just called the police **when** the doorbell rang.

Fertig?

1 Paare

Welche Satzteile passen zusammen? Bilde aus folgenden Satzhälften einen vollen Satz!

Which sentences match? Match up the sentence halves to make whole sentences.

1. Wir waren gerade aus dem Zug ausgestiegen,
2. Mutter hatte gerade die Pizza aus dem Ofen genommen,
3. Gudrun war gerade aus Italien heimgekommen,
4. Ich hatte gerade mein Fahrrad geputzt,
5. Georg und Matthias hatten gerade ihre Mäntel abgelegt,

a. als ihre Austauschpartnerin anrief.
b. als es wieder zu regnen begann.
c. als wir die Lautsprecherdurchsage hörten.
d. als der Hund ein Stück davon klaute.
e. als ich durch den Schlamm fahren musste.

Ⓗ 2 Gestern

Gestern ist Claudia Krall bei folgenden Personen eingebrochen. Was hatten sie gemacht, bevor sie nach Hause kamen? Schreibe Sätze zu den Bildern!

Claudia Krall burgled the houses of these people yesterday. What had these people been doing before they got home? Write captions for the pictures.

1. Frau Springs

eine Zeitung lesen;
im Café

2. Angela und Petra

zusammen Squash spielen;
im Fitness-Zentrum

3. Roland

einen Aufsatz schreiben;
in der Schule

4. Herr Beckmann

Blumen für seine Frau kaufen

5. Christoph

mit dem Zug; von Bremen
fahren

H *3 Das gehört nicht dazu*
Finde die falsch geschriebenen Verbformen und korrigiere sie!

Identify which verb forms are incorrect, and correct them.

1. Jürgen hattet ein schönes Bild in Aquarell bemalt.
2. Die Familie Beckstein hatte nach Australien gefahrt.
3. Die Nachrichten warst ganz schlecht gewesen.
4. Herr Meckel hatte im Lotto sehr viel Geld gewinnen.
5. Hendrik hatten seinen Onkel in Potsdam besucht.
6. Ich hatte einen Liebesbrief bekommt.
7. Wir hatten uns Eiscreme gekauft.
8. Es war zu schneien angefangen.

Los!

⊞ *4 Bankküberfall*

Stelle dir vor, dass du gerade einen Bankküberfall gesehen hast! Beschreibe der Polizei, was passiert ist! Verwende verschiedene Vergangenheitsformen!

Imagine you have just seen a bank robbery. Describe to the police what you saw, using a mixture of past tenses.

⊞ *5 Bankküberfall – in Echt!*

Eine Wiederholung von Übung 4, nur, dass du jetzt einen Bericht von einem wahren Überfall, aus der Zeitung, schreiben sollst.

This is a repeat of Exercise 4, except that you should now write a report of a real robbery, based on a newspaper story.

GLOSSAR

die Lautsprecherdurchsage	loudspeaker announcement
ablegen (sep.)	to take off
der Schlamm	mud
der Bankküberfall	bank robbery
sich vorstellen	to imagine
Aquarelle	watercolour paints
der Aufsatz	essay

33

WRITE! RIGHT?

Spelling matters

 Auf die Plätze!

Spelling and meaning

The **spelling** of any word, not just a noun, can seriously affect its **meaning**, thus:

Um wie viel Uhr kommen sie?	When are **they** coming?
Um wie viel Uhr kommen Sie?	When are **you** coming?
	(formal 'you')
Wein gefällt uns gut.	We like **wine**.
Wien gefällt uns gut.	We like **Vienna**!
Wir bleiben nicht lange.	We **are** not staying for long.
	(present tense)
Wir blieben nicht lange.	We **did** not stay for long.
	(imperfect tense)

 Toller Tipp!

This may seem daunting, but German has the great advantage of spelling its words exactly as a German says them: there are no silent sounds or endings! So, regular practice, aloud, preferably with your teacher or a native speaker, like an Assistent(in), will help.

Reading new vocabulary aloud while you write it out, is the best way to learn it thoroughly.

At home, when you may not have a partner to help you, you could always **record it on cassette. Repeated listening** is often easier than just speaking and writing practice.

Grammatik Aktiv!

1 Letters, and sounds and things
a The German Alphabet

So, here is the **German alphabet**, with its nearest phonetic spelling in an English 'equivalent' and the IPA (International Phonetic Alphabet) symbol [in brackets] alongside:

a	ah	[a]	*n*	enn	[en]
b	beh	[be]	*o*	oh	[o]
c	tseh	[tse]	*p*	peh	[pe]
d	deh	[de]	*q*	coo	[ku]
e	eh	[e]	*r*	air	[ɛR]
f	eff	[ɛf]	*s*	ess	[ɛs]
g	geh	[ge]	*t*	teh	[te]
h	hah	[ha]	*u*	oo	[u]
i	ee	[i]	*v*	fow	[fau]
j	yot	[jot]	*w*	veh	[ve]
k	kah	[ka]	*x*	ix	[Ix]
l	ell	[ɛl]	*y*	oopsilon	[ypsǝlon]
m	emm	[ɛm]	*z*	tsett	[tsɛt]

b Dipthongs and Umlauts

Diphthongs			**Umlaut**		
aa	ah	[a]	*ä*	eh	[e]
ai	eye	[ai]			
au	ow!	[au]	*äu*	oy	[oy]
ee	eh	[e]			
ei	eye	[ai]			
eu	oy	[oy]			
ie	ee	[i]			
oo	oh	[o]	*ö*	euh!	[ø]
ü	ew*	[y]	(* as in ewe/few)		

c Sounds and Spelling

Punctuation and more spelling. You might now like to look more carefully at the sounds and their relationship to spelling.

■ *a* can be 'long' *ah* [a]:   *wir fahren; ich habe*
   The following *-h* automatically **lengthens** vowels.
   or
   a can be 'short' *a* [a]:   *Was ist das?; Kannst du Basketball* spielen?
   [baskɛtbal]

A following **double consonant** (-*nn*, -*ll*) **shortens** the vowel.

■ *b* is pronounced like an English 'b' [b] at the **beginning** of a word or **in the middle**, before a vowel:
Bringst *du mich ins* **B**üro? [byro]
*Was ha***b***en wir heute A***b***end vor?* [abɛnt]

but like a *p* [p] at the **end of words** or **before consonants**:
*Was ha***b***t ihr a***b *nächster Woche vor?* [hapt]
Gi***b*** *mir ein Stück O***b***st.* [opst]

■ *c* is rare, but generally pronounced like *k* [k]:
das **C**afé, **C**ola, *die* **C**urrywurst. [kafe]

But, as a **foreign**, **borrowed letter**, it is normally pronounced as in the original language:
Capu**cc**ino (Italian), **Ch**ef (French), **C**D (English), [kaputʒino]
Center (U.S. English) [tsɛnta]

NB: however: *Mer***c***edes!* [mɛRtsedes]

■ *ch* is an important native German sound, whose standard pronunciation is like the Scots Gaelic 'Lo**ch**' [ç]:
i**ch**, a**ch**!, a**ch**tzehn, ri**ch**tig! [açtsen]; [RIçtIç]

but, before -*s* it is generally pronounced 'hard' like a *k*:
se**chs**, wa**chs**en, [zɛks]; [vaksɛn]

■ *d* is like the hard English sound at the beginning of a word or between vowels:
Dürfen mein Bru***d***er und ich eine **D**usche nehmen? [dyRfɛn]; [duʒɛ]

but it sounds like a -*t* at the end or before a consonant:
Han***d***, Freiba***d***, die Sta***d***t, die Lan***d***schaft, das Lan***d*** [hant]

■ *e* can be 'short' [e] between consonants and is always short before a double consonant:
essen, spr***e***chen, d***e***r, d***e***s, **E**lbe, **E**nde [ɛsɛn]; [ʒpRɛçɛn]

or 'long' [e] before -*m*, -*n*, or a single consonant followed by another vowel:
d***e***m, d***e***n, l***e***sen, s***e***hen [dem]; [ze:ɛn].

■ *f* and *v* are both pronounced as an English 'ff' [f]:
finden, wie **v**iel, **F**oto, **V**olkswagen, dar**f**, TÜ**V** [vifil]; [folksvagɛn]

■ *g* is 'hard' [g] at the **beginning** or in the **middle** of words:
gehen, **g**ut, Mitta**g**essen, **G**rüß **G**ott! [ge:ɛn]; [mItagɛsɛn]

but 'whispered' like -*ch* after *i*- at the end of words, especially numbers and adjectives:
sechzig, richtig   [zɛ çtsIç]; [RIçtIç]

However, it is pronounced like *k* [k] at the **ends** of words **after a vowel**:
mag, flog, Flugzeug   [mak]; [fluk:tsoyk]

It is pronounced as in standard English **after *n*-,** [ŋ]:
singen, lang, eng, England   [zIŋɛn]; [eŋlant]

- *h* is **pronounced** as **clearly** as in correct English at the **beginning** of words:
*h*ast, *h*ören, *h*undert

Importantly, it **lengthens vowels** in the **middle or at the end** of words, where it marks a '**glottal stop**':
sah, fahren, sehen, Ruhe!, früh.   [Ru:ə]; [fRy]

- *i* is 'short' [I] when alone **without another vowel**:
bist, Kinder, ich   [KIndɛR]; [Iç]

It is 'long' [i] only in foreign 'loan' words:
Vitamine, Kiwifrüchte   [vItamine]; [kivifRYçtə]

- *j* is like the English 'y' [j]:
Joghurt, **j**a!, **j**eder   [ja]; [jedɛR]

- *k* is pronounced like its English equivalent [k]. In German it is **much more normal than** the foreign letter 'c':
klar, aktiv, Kultur, sinken   [aktif]; [zInkɛn]

- *l, m, n* are exactly as in English:
lernen, Hallo!, toll   [lɛRnɛn]; [tol]
Musik, Grammatik, dem   [muzik]; [gramatIk]
nicht, sonnig, begann   [nIçt]; [zonIç]

- *o* is generally 'long' [o] and always so **before -*h***:
also, hoch, wohnen, Montag, Brot   [hoç]; [montak]

but it is sometimes 'short' [o] and always so before a **double consonant**:
Donnerstag, Mittwoch, toll, kosten   [donɛRstak]; [mItvoç]

- *p* is like the English equivalent [p]:
Polizei, Cam**p**ing**p**latz, Su**pp**e, kna**pp**   [polItsai]; [zʊpɛ]

- *q* is always followed by -*u*-, but pronounced as [kv]:
Quark, be**qu**em, **qu**ietschen   [kvaRk]; [bɛkvem]

- *r* has a **guttural** pronunciation [R] in modern standard German, as in French:
Freitag, Ruhe!, Herr   [fRaitak]; [Ru:e]

■ *s* is 'hard' [z] when **alone before a vowel**:
sollen, lesen, leise, Musik

[laizɛ]; [muzik]

s is 'soft' [s] when doubled or **before a consonant**:
los!, Mist!, der beste, müssen

[los]; [mYsɛn]

s is pronounced like the English 'sh-' [ζ], **before -*t* and -*p* at the beginning of words**:
sp*ielen*, st*ehen*, St*uttgart*, Sp*anien*

[ζpilɛn]; [ζte:ɛn]

or when such words carry a *prefix* before them:
ver*stehen*, aus*steigen*

[fɛrζte:ən]; [ausζtaigən]

s makes the same sound 'sh-' when added to -*ch* [ç]:
Sch*ade!*, Du*sche*, fri*sch*

[ζadɛ]; [fRiζ]

NB: Ski, or Schi, is **always** prounounced as: [ζi]

■ *ß* replaces a double -*ss*- with the **same pronunciation**, in the following situation:

ONLY when the **preceeding vowel sound, including umlaut or diphthong** is **long**:
*s*ü*ß*, *hei*ß*t*, *gro*ß, *Fü*ß*e*

[zys]; [fyse]

but **not** when the vowel, including umlaut, is short:
müsst, *verlässt*, *der Fluss*, *die Flüsse*

[fɛRlɛst]; [f lYsɛ]

 Pass Auf!

SWISS GERMAN tends not to use *ß*.

Until August 1998 *ß* was always used:

i. **before a consonant**:

du mußt, er heißt, was paßt am besten?

[mʊst]; [haist]

ii. at the **end of a word**:

ich muß, es ist heiß!, das ist süß!

[hais]; [zys]

iii. in the **middle of a word after a long** (not a *short**) **vowel** sound:

Süßigkeiten, wie heißen Sie?, welche Größe

[sYsIçkaitɛn];[gRøsɛ]

but compare * *wir müssen, geschlossen, das Kopfkissen*

■ *t* is like its English equivalent in most positions:
Stadtmitte, *Tischtennis*, *Boot*

[ζtatmItɛ]; [bot]

but in the combination **-tion**, it is pronounced like -z [ts]:
*interna**tion**al, U-Bahnsta**tion*** [uban ʦatsion]

■ ***u*** is pronounced either 'long', as in English 'oo' [u]:
*R**u**he!, B**u**ch, **U**h**u*** [Ru:e]; [buç]

or 'short' [ʊ] as in northern English pronunciation:
*M**u**tter, du m**u**sst, d**u**mm!* [mʊter]; [dʊm]

■ ***ü*** similarly, and importantly for the spelling -ss- or -ß-, can be 'long':
*s**ü**ß, eine T**ü**te, die Sp**ü**lmaschine* [zy:s]; [ʃpy:lmaʦinɛ]

or 'short':
*wir m**ü**ssen, M**ü**nchen, Fl**ü**sse* [mYnçen]; [f lYsɛ]

■ ***v*** as previously shown, is pronounced like *ff* [f] (see above: *f*):
***V**olkswagen, wie **v**iel, akti**v**!* [vifil]; [aktif]

■ ***w*** on the other hand, is pronounced like *v* [v]. Take care in practising:
*Volks**w**agen, **w**ie viel, U**w**e, **W**urst!* [folksvagɛn]; [vuRst]

■ ***x*** is as *rare* as in English and is pronounced the same way [ks]:
*se**x**istisch, Ma**x**, Fa**x**maschine* [faksmaʦine]

■ ***y*** is pronounced like a 'long' *ü*, unlike any sound in English:
*t**y**pisch, Ph**y**sik, S**y**stem* [tYpIʦ]; [zYstem]

■ ***z*** is pronounced as *ts* [ts] and must not be confused with *s* [z]:
***Z**ug, **z**wischen, kur**z**, **z**wan**z**ig* [tsuk]; [tsvantsiç]

👀 Pass auf!

Compare:				
	(i)	*mein **Z**ahn*	my tooth	[tsan]
		*meine **S**ahne*	my cream	[zane]
	(ii)	*drei**z**ehn*	thirteen	[dRaitsen]
		*drei**ß**ig*	thirty	[dRaisIç]

2 Say it right = get it right! Right? Write!

To pronounce the sounds correctly you must **spell** them correctly.
The opening examples showed how important this is in German in particular.
For German vowel combinations (**diphthongs**) and sound-changes (**umlaut**) this is
especially true!

■ Adding an **umlaut** (*a/ä; o/ö; u/ü*) means a **complete change of sound**, which
often changes the **meaning** from:

a singular to plural

*ein M*a*nn*	[man]	*zwei M*ä*nner*	[mɛnɛR]
*eine W*a*nd*	[vant]	*vier W*ä*nde*	[vɛndɛ]

b one **verb form** to another

*du m*u*sst*	[must]	*ihr m*ü*sst*	[mYst]

c one **tense** to another

*du k*o*nntest*	[kontɛst]	you **were** able to..	(imperfect tense)
*du k*ö*nntest*	[køntɛst]	you **would be** able to…	
			(conditional tense)

d one **word** to a quite different one

*wir f*u*hren*	[fuRɛn]	we travelled/drove
*wir f*ü*hren*	[fYRɛn]	we lead/manage

e a simple adjective to a comparative/superlative-

ein junger Mann	[juŋɛR]	a young man
*ein j*ü*nger***er** *Mann*	[jYŋɛRɛR]	a young**er** man

■ The **diphthongs -ie-** [i] and **-ei-** [ai] have a totally **different sound** from each other:

*d*ie*se, d*ie*, fl*ie*gen, W*ie*n*	[dise],[di], [fligen], [vin]

contrast with: *m*ei*n, w*ei*t, h*ei*ßen, W*ei*ßwein*   [main], [vait], [haisen],[vaisvain]

■ This change of sound can also indicate a change of:

a tense	*wir schr*ei*ben*	[ʒ raiben] we are writing	(present tense)
	*wir schr*ie*ben*	[ʒrib∂n] we wrote	(imperfect tense)

b meaning	*die drei W*ei*sen*	[vais∂n]	the three **wise men**
	*die drei W*ie*sen*	[vis∂n]	the three **fields/meadows**
	*Danke, das r*ei*cht!*	[Raiçt]]	Thank you: that**'s enough.**
	*Danke, das r*ie*cht!*	[Riçt]	No thanks: it **smells**!
	*R*ei*chen Sie mir das, bitte!*	Please **pass** that to me.	
	*R*ie*chen Sie das mal, bitte!*	Please **smell** that for me!	

Fertig?

1 Was fehlt?

Fülle folgende Lücken mit den passenden Buchstaben aus! Vorsicht mit der Rechtschreibung! Sprich erstmals jedes Wort laut aus!

Fill in the following gaps with the appropriate letters. Check your spelling. Say every word aloud first.

1. Ich h—ße Uwe. M—n H—s l—gt in W—n.
2. W— gef-llt dir d—ser Rotw—n?
3. K—nnten –ie mir bitte d— Sp—sekarte r—chen?
4. Als m—ne Frau v—l j-nger war, h—ß sie Fr—lein Bäcker.
   Jetzt h—ßt -ie Fr— Müller!
5. Ulli! Du m-sst mir helfen ! Alle W-nde m—ner H—ser m-ssen
   wir renovieren!
6. Ich bin -lter als du: k-nntest du bitte auf d— L—ter
   st—gen?

2 Wie schreibt man das?

Schreibe folgende Worte nach ihrer phonetischen Schreibweise ins normale Deutsch um!

Write out the following sentences in normal German, using their phonetic transcripts.

1. [vi] [haist] [du]?
2. [main] [hous] [likt] [tsviζ∂n] [win] [unt] [zaltsbuRk].
3. [iç] [von∂] [In] [dɛR] [ne:ɛ] [fon] [dɛR] [ζvaits].
4. [als] [iç] [jYŋɛR] [vaR], [mustɛ] [iç] [vil] [ζRaibɛn].
5. [viR] [Raizɛn] [libɛR] [mIt] [dem] [fluktsoyk] [naç] [doytζland]
   [als] [mIt] [dem] [tsuk].

Los!

3 Schreib's auf!
Am rechten Rand der letzten beiden Kapitel findest du viele Beispiele in phonetischer Schreibweise. Decke erstmals die linke Seite zu und versuche das phonetische ins normale Deutsch umzuschreiben!

On the right-hand side of the pages in the last two units you will see many phonetic transcriptions of the words used as examples. Now cover the left-hand side and try to transcribe the phonetics into their normal German form.

H 4 Und jetzt, der Rest!
Nicht alle Beispiele sind in phonetischer Form umgeschrieben worden. Schreibe jetzt die restlichen Beispiele aus dem normalen Deutsch in die phonetische Form um!

Not all of the examples have been transcribed into their phonetic form. Now write the remaining examples in phonetic transcript.

5 Diktat!
Diktiere deinem Partner bzw. deiner Gruppe einen Satz aus den 'Fertig'-Übungen (oben)! Jeder, der zuhört, muss den Satz aufschreiben! Tauscht dann die Rollen! Kontrolliert die Rechtschreibung der Anderen!

Dictate one of the sentences from the 'Fertig' exercise to you partner or your group. Everyone listening must write down the sentence. Now change roles. Check each other's spelling.

6 Wie heißt du? Wie schreibt man das?
Führe einen Dialog mit deinem Partner! Erkläre deinen Namen, deinen Wohnort, deine Adresse usw. Buchstabiere alle Namen!

Hold a conversation with a partner, state your name, your home town, your address, etc. Spell out all the names.

7 Hör gut zu!
Kein Partner? Nimm die Sätze auf Kassette auf! Später kann dein Partner bzw. dein Lehrer das alles kontrollieren.

No partner? Record it all onto cassette. Your partner or teacher can then check it all later.

34

PUNCTUATE IT!
Full-stops, commas, !, etc.

 Auf die Plätze!

Interpunktion bzw. Zeichensetzung
German punctuation follows stricter grammatical and syntactic rules than English:

1 Full stop (Punkt)

- This not only **ends a sentence**.

- It also marks **an abbreviated ending** after **dates** and **ordinal numbers**.

- It separates **thousands** (not decimal places)!

- German also uses a full stop to indicate its many **abbreviated expressions**, often in business letters:

Betr. Besuch am 7.05.2001   Hamburg, den 2. Mai.

Sehr geehrte Herren,

laut Ihres Faxes vom 30.4. besuchen Sie unsere Fabrik am 7. d. M.
Dort produzieren wir z.Z. 2.000 Maschinen mit einem Umsatz von
ca. 6,5 Mio Euro.

... Wenn Sie mehr Zeit hätten, könnten Sie unsere Büros in Plymouth
bzw. Dartmouth u.a. besuchen, um unsere Arbeitsmethoden näher kennen
zu lernen. Faxen Sie uns bitte die Zahl der Herren ggf. der Damen,
die Sie begleiten sollen. Wir wünschen gute Reise!

Mit freundlichen Grüßen,

i.A ....
(Müller)

---

2 Commas

■ You will notice above that, unlike the English, Germans (like other continentals) **use commas to denote a decimal point**.

■ Most importantly, **commas** mark not a pause, but the **division** between one **clause** (e.g. main clause) and another (e.g. sub-clause).

Beispiel:

Ich muss Deutsch lernen, weil ich morgen eine Klassenarbeit schreibe.
Wenn ich nach England fliege, nehme ich immer Reisetabletten.

3 Exclamation marks

These are expected when you:

a Begin a greeting

Lieber Klaus!, *Alles Gute!*

b Give a command

Pass auf!, *Setzen Sie sich!*

 **Fertig?**

1 Ein totales Durcheinander!

Dein Fax hat folgendes gedruckt! Schreibe oder tippe den ganzen Brief in richtiger Form, d.h. mit voller Interpunktion und Rechtschreibung! Vorsicht: deine englische Faxmaschine hat keine Möglichkeit, Umlaute und ß einzusetzen. Viel Spaß!

Your fax has printed the following! Write or type the whole letter out correctly, making sure you use correct punctuation and spelling. Be careful: your English fax machine does not have the capability to recognise *umlauts* or *ß*! Have fun!

```
kolnden24marz1999sehrgeehrterherrthompsonichbedankemichhe
rzlichfurihrenbriefderunsgesternerreichthatwennichsierich
tigverstehemochtensieundihrekollegenunserburoam30marzbesu
chenichglaubeleidernichtdasswirsiediesmalbegrussenkonnenw
eilunserefabrikgeschlossenistichmochteihnenaberfolgendenv
orschlagmachenkommensiedochselbermitihrerfraubzwihrersekr
etarinwennsiezeithattenkonnteichihnenmeinestadtzeigenwasm
einensiedazudenrheinundseinenweinmussensiedochnaherkennen
lernenichwunscheihneneinegutereiseundvielspassinkolnmitfr
eundlichengrussenmuller.
```

205

Los!

H *2 Wörterbuchübung!*

Schlag im Wörterbuch nach! Schreibe alle Kurzformen aus dem Geschäftsbrief auf Seite 204 in voll aus!

Use a dictionary to help you write out in full all the abbreviations in the business letter on P.204.

Beispiel:

z.B. = zum Beispiel!

35

WHAT'S NEW?

Spelling reforms

 **Auf die Plätze!**

Deutsches Wörterbuch in der Hand; was ist jetzt richtig im ganzen Land?
Rechtschreibreform – Spelling reforms 1998 – 2004/5.
There is no doubt that German spelling today is more uniform than in Martin
Luther's or Mozart's day! However, note the following:

a. Swiss German does not use the letter *ß*, in any position

b. Printed documents sometimes write *-ae-, -oe-, -ue-* instead of -ä-, -ö-, -ü-
respectively.

c. Since the **spelling reforms**, the following changes should have been accepted in
all of the Federal States of Germany as well as elsewhere. Meanwhile, 'old' spellings
should be tolerated until 2004/5.

The reforms worth noting for GCSE/Scottish Standard level, since they are
generally not optional, include:

■ **Doubling consonants, where this is logical, or tripling them, logically,
when two words are combined.**

■ **Writing *-ß-* ONLY after long vowel sounds, in whichever position:**
   heiß, heißt, Fuß   BUT   *dass, musst, Fluss*

■ **Separating words in compound verbs or other combinations where each
separate part has a meaning on its own:**
   Staub saugen   BUT   *schwerstbehindert*

■ **Using capital initial letters for all nouns, including set phrases and adjectival nouns:**

alles Gute! Das Beste im Westen! Die Grünen.

■ **Using only small case letters for all adjectives, unless in official titles:**

auf Englisch, die erste Hilfe   BUT   *das Rote Kreuz*

■ **Simplifying spelling where letters are not pronounced (e.g. imported foreign 'loan' words):**

Tunfisch/Thunfisch, Delfin/Delphin

■ **Always spelling d*u* and i*hr* with small initial letters, even when addressing friends in letters, postcards etc:**

Liebe Ulli,
*wie geht's **d**ir und **d**einer Familie? ...*

 ## Fertig?

⊞ *1 Das ist neu!*

Für jede Kategorie der oben angegebenen Reformen findest du unten konkrete Beispiele.
Fülle die Lücken mit den neuen Schreibformen aus! Vorsicht: nicht alle müssen sich ändern!

For each of the above categories of spelling reforms you will find concrete examples below. Fill in the remaining gaps. Beware: some will not change.

A.

– 1998	1998 +
1. Nummer (n.)	nummerieren (vb.)
2. ... (n.)	tippen (vb.)
3. Schiff + Fahrt	Schifffahrt
4. Kunststoff + Flasche	...
5. daß	dass (short vowel)
6. muß	... (short vowel)
7. süß	süß (long vowel)
8. heißen	... (diphthong)
9. ihr müßt	... (short vowel)
10. du verläßt	... (short vowel)

B.

1.	staubsaugen	Staub* saugen (noun*)
2.	radfahren	…
3.	sitzenbleiben	sitzen bleiben (2 verbs)
4.	spazierengehen	… …
5.	kennenlernen	… …
6.	obenerwähnt	oben* erwähnt (adverb*)
7.	rotgestreift	… … (adjective)
8.	hartgekocht	… … (adjective)
9.	soviel	so viel (adverb/adj.)
10.	wieviel ?	… …

C.

1.	heute morgen	heute Morgen * (noun*)
2.	gestern abend	… …
3.	im großen und ganzen	im Großen und Ganzen*
4.	im allgemeinen	… … (*adj.noun)
5.	das beste	das Beste (adj.noun)
6.	auf deutsch	… …
7.	Erste Hilfe	erste* Hilfe (adjective*)
8.	das Schwarze* Brett	… … …
9.	das erstemal	das erste Mal * (noun*)
10.	jedesmal	… …

D.

1.	Mikrophon	Mikrophon/Mikrofon
2.	**Ph**otogra**ph**ie	…
3.	Tele**ph**on	…
4.	Del**ph**in	…
5.	Ket**ch**up	Ketchup/…
6.	**Th**unfisch	Thunfisch/**Tun**fisch
7.	Jo**gh**urt	Jog**h**urt/… (silent **h**)
8.	Kän**gh**uru	…
9.	F**ö**n	der F**öh**n (**-h** lengthens)
10.	selbständig	**selbst**ständig (selbst exist alone)

36

APPENDIX I
German verb forms

Irregular verbs: haben – *to have*, sein – *to be*, werden – *to become*

Imperative – have!, be!, become! etc.		
habe!	*sei!*	*werde!*
habt!	*seid!*	*werdet!*
haben Sie!	*seien Sie!*	*werden Sie!*

Present tense – I have, am, become etc.			
ich	*habe*	*bin*	*werde*
du	*hast*	*bist*	*wirst*
er/sie/es/man	*hat*	*ist*	*wird*
wir	*haben*	*sind*	*werden*
ihr	*habt*	*seid*	*werdet*
sie/Sie	*haben*	*sind*	*werden*

Imperfect tense – I had/was having, was, became			
ich	*hatte*	*war*	*wurde*
du	*hattest*	*warst*	*wurdest*
er/sie/es/man	*hatte*	*war*	*wurde*
wir	*hatten*	*waren*	*wurden*
ihr	*hattet*	*wart*	*wurdet*
sie/Sie	*hatten*	*waren*	*wurden*

Perfect tense – I had/did have, was/have been, became/have become etc.		
ich habe gehabt	*ich bin gewesen*	*ich bin geworden*

Pluperfect tense – I had had, had been, had become etc.		
ich hatte gehabt	*ich war gewesen*	*ich war geworden*

Future tense – I will have, will be, will become etc.

ich werde haben	*ich werde sein*	*ich werde werden*

Subjunctive (present/imperfect) – see Chapter 31 for translations

habe/hätte	*sei/wäre*	*werde/würde*

Conditional – I would have, would be, would become etc.

ich würde haben	*ich würde sein*	*ich würde werden*

Regular weak and strong verbs: e.g. *machen* – to make, do; *schlafen* – to sleep

Imperative – make! sleep! etc.

	mache!	*schlafe!*
	macht!	*schlaft!*
	machen Sie!	*schlafen Sie!*

Present tense – I make, sleep etc.

ich	*mache*	*schlafe*
du	*machst*	*schläfst*
er/sie/es/man	*macht*	*schläft*
wir	*machen*	*schlafen*
ihr	*macht*	*schlaft*
sie/Sie	*machen*	*schlafen*

Imperfect tense – I made/was making, slept/was sleeping etc.

ich	*machte*	*schlief*
du	*machtest*	*schliefst*
er/sie/es/man	*machte*	*schlief*
wir	*machten*	*schliefen*
ihr	*machtet*	*schlieft*
sie/Sie	*machten*	*schliefen*

Perfect tense – I made/have made, slept/have slept etc.

ich habe gemacht	*ich habe geschlafen usw.*

Grammatik Aktiv!

Pluperfect tense – I had made, had slept etc.

ich hatte gemacht   *ich hatte geschlafen usw.*

Future tense – I will make, will sleep etc.

ich werde machen   *ich werde schlafen*

Subjunctive – See Chapter 31

mache/machte   *schlafe/schliefe*

Conditional – I would make, would sleep etc.

ich würde machen   *ich würde schlafen*

Modal verbs: *können* – to be able to

Present tense – I can etc.

ich	*kann*	also
du	*kannst*	*dürfen:* to be allowed – *ich darf, du darfst*
er/sie/es/man	*kann*	*mögen:* to like – *ich mag, du magst*
wir	*können*	*müssen:* to have to – *ich muss, du musst*
ihr	*könnt*	*sollen:* to ought to – *ich soll, du sollst*
sie/Sie	*können*	*wollen:* to want to – *ich will, du willst*

Imperfect tense – I could etc.

ich	*konnte*	
du	*konntest*	*ich durfte, du durftest*
er/sie/es/man	*konnte*	*ich mochte, du mochtest*
wir	*konnten*	*ich musste, du musstest*
ihr	*konntet*	*ich sollte, du solltest*
sie/Sie	*konnten*	*ich wollte, du wolltest*

Perfect tense – I have been able etc.

ich habe gekonnt*	*gedurft*
	gemocht
	gemusst
	gesollt
	gewollt

Pluperfect tense – I had been able etc.

---

ich hatte gekonnt

Future tense – I will be able etc.

---

ich werde können

Subjunctive (present/imperfect) – See Chapter 29

---

könne/könnte	*dürfe/dürfte*
solle/sollte	*möge/möchte*
wolle/wollte	*müsse/müsste*

Conditional – I would be able etc.

---

ich würde können

---

* In fact, the past participle of modals is rarely used, whenever another infinitive is in the same sentence:

> *Ich habe diese TV – Sendung sehen wollen* (NOT *gewollt*)
> I wanted to see this TV programme.

Verbs which use sein as an auxiliary: e.g. *fahren* – to go, travel

---

Perfect tense – I went/ have gone etc.

---

ich bin gefahren
du bist gefahren
er/sie/es ist gefahren
wir sind gefahren
ihr seid gefahren
sie/Sie sind gefahren

Pluperfect tense – I had gone etc.

---

ich war gefahren
du warst gefahren
er/sie/es war gefahren
wir waren gefahren
ihr wart gefahren
sie/Sie waren gefahren

Grammatik Aktiv!

Reflexive verbs & their pronouns: *sich setzen* – to sit down

Present tense – I sit down etc.		
ich	*setze*	**mich**
du	*setzst*	**dich**
er/sie/es/man	*setzt*	**sich**
wir	*setzen*	**uns**
ihr	*setzt*	**euch**
sie/Sie	*setzen*	**sich**

Principal forms of strong/irregular verbs

■ The following table lists the principal parts of the commonest strong or irregular German verbs. In most cases it is the *er/sie/es* (3rd person singular) form which is given. With very few exceptions you can use these to work out the other weak forms; except for a very small number of highly irregular verbs, the *wir*, *ihr* and *sie/Sie* (plural) forms are always regular.

■ For verbs with a prefix, look for the root verb, e.g. *an***greifen**.

■ * shows that this verb takes *sein* (not *haben*), in the perfect and pluperfect tenses:

e.g. *er **ist** geblieben* etc. he has stayed (NOT *er hat geblieben*).

■ Some shorthand codes: + dat. = dative object; *jdn.* = *jemanden* (accusative); *jdm.* = *jemandem* (dative) somebody; sb. = somebody; *etw.* = *etwas*/something;

Infinitive		Present	Imperfect	Past Participle	Notes
befehlen	to order	*befiehlt*	*befahl*	*befohlen*	+ dat.
beginnen	to begin	*beginnt*	*begann*	*begonnen*	
bekommen	to receive	*bekommt*	*bekam*	*bekommen*	
bieten	to offer	*bietet*	*bot*	*geboten*	*an jdn.* – to sb.
bitten	to request	*bittet*	*bat*	*gebeten*	
bleiben	to stay, remain	*bleibt*	*blieb*	*geblieben**	
bringen	to bring	*bringt*	*brachte*	*gebracht*	
denken	to think	*denkt*	*dachte*	*gedacht*	*an etw.* – about sth.
empfehlen	to recommend	*empfiehlt*	*empfahl*	*empfohlen*	+ dat.
entscheiden	to decide	*entscheidet*	*entschied*	*entschieden*	
essen	to eat	*isst*	*aß*	*gegessen*	
fahren	to go, travel	*fährt*	*fuhr*	*gefahren**	*ab-* – depart
fallen	to fall	*fällt*	*fiel*	*gefallen**	
finden	to find	*findet*	*fand*	*gefunden*	*statt-* – take place
fliegen	to fly	*fliegt*	*flog*	*geflogen**	
geben	to give	*gibt*	*gab*	*gegeben*	*jdm etw.* – sb. sth.
gehen	to go (on foot)	*geht*	*ging*	*gegangen**	*spazieren-* – stroll
gewinnen	to win	*gewinnt*	*gewann*	*gewonnen*	
haben	to have	*hat*	*hatte*	*gehabt*	
halten	to stop, hold	*hält*	*hielt*	*gehalten*	
heißen	to be called	*heißt*	*hieß*	*geheißen*	
helfen	to help	*hilft*	*half*	*geholfen*	+ dat.
kennen	to know (person)	*kennt*	*kannte*	*gekannt*	
kommen	to come	*kommt*	*kam*	*gekommen**	*an-* – arrive

Grammatik Aktiv!

Infinitive		Present	Imperfect	Past Participle	Notes
lassen	to allow	*lässt*	*ließ*	*gelassen*	*ver-* – leave
laufen	to run	*läuft*	*lief*	*gelaufen**	
lesen	to read	*liest*	*las*	*gelesen*	*vor-* – read out
liegen	to lie	*liegt*	*lag*	*gelegen*	
nehmen	to take	*nimmt*	*nahm*	*genommen*	*teil-* – take part
nennen	to name	*nennt*	*nannte*	*genannt*	
rufen	to call	*ruft*	*rief*	*gerufen*	an- telephone
schlafen	to sleep	*schläft*	*schlief*	*geschlafen*	*ein- fall asleep
schlagen	to hit, strike	*schlägt*	*schlug*	*geschlagen*	
schließen	to close	*schließt*	*schloss*	*geschlossen*	
schreiben	to write	*schreibt*	*schrieb*	*geschrieben*	
schreien	to shout	*schreit*	*schrie*	*geschri[e]n*	
schwimmen	to swim	*schwimmt*	*schwamm*	*geschwommen**	
sehen	to see	*sieht*	*sah*	*gesehen*	*fern-* – watch TV
sein	to be	*ist*	*war*	*gewesen**	
sitzen	to sit	*sitzt*	*saß*	*gesessen*	
sprechen	to speak	*spricht*	*sprach*	*gesprochen*	
springen	to jump	*springt*	*sprang*	*gesprungen**	
stehen	to stand	*steht*	*stand*	*gestanden*	**auf-* – get up
sterben	to die	*stirbt*	*starb*	*gestorben**	
tragen	to carry; wear	*trägt*	*trug*	*getragen*	
treffen	to meet; hit	*trifft*	*traf*	*getroffen*	
trinken	to drink	*trinkt*	*trank*	*getrunken*	
tun	to do	*tut*	*tat*	*getan*	
vergessen	to forget	*vergisst*	*vergaß*	*vergessen*	
verlieren	to lose	*verliert*	*verlor*	*verloren*	
wachsen	to grow	*wächst*	*wuchs*	*gewachsen**	
waschen	to wash	*wäscht*	*wusch*	*gewaschen*	
werfen	to throw	*wirft*	*warf*	*geworfen*	
werden	to become	*wird*	*wurde*	*geworden**	
wissen	to know (fact)	*weiß*	*wusste*	*gewusst*	
ziehen	to pull	*zieht*	*zog*	*gezogen*	*aus-* – undress; **um-* – move house

Modal verbs
See Chapter 17 for more information about this special group of verbs.

Infinitive		Present	Imperfect	Past Participle
dürfen	to be allowed to	*darf*	*durfte*	*dürfen, gedurft*
können	to be able to	*kann*	*konnte*	*können, gekonnt*
mögen	to like (to)	*mag*	*mochte*	*mögen, gemocht*
müssen	to have to	*muss*	*musste*	*müssen, gemusst*
sollen	to ought to	*soll*	*sollte*	*sollen, gesollt*
wollen	to want to	*will*	*wollte*	*wollen, gewollt*

37

APPENDIX II
tables

1 Pronouns

Personal pronouns

	I	you	he	she	it	one	we	you (pl)	they	you (polite)
Nominative	*ich*	*du*	*er*	*sie*	*es*	*man*	*wir*	*ihr*	*sie*	*Sie*
Accusative	*mich*	*dich*	*ihn*	*sie*	*es*	*einen*	*uns*	*euch*	*sie*	*Sie*
Dative	*mir*	*dir*	*ihm*	*ihr*	*ihm*	*einem*	*uns*	*euch*	*ihnen*	*Ihnen*

Reflexive pronouns
see Chapter 20: Reflexive Verbs

	myself	yourself	himself/ herself itself/ oneself	ourselves yourself	yourselves	themselves	yourself (polite)
Accusative	*mich*	*dich*	*sich*	*uns*	*euch*	*sich*	*sich*
Dative	*mir*	*dir*	*sich*	*uns*	*euch*	*sich*	*sich*

Possessive pronouns
see Chapter 6: Possessive Pronouns; and Chapter 28: Adjectival Endings

my	your(s)	his	her	its	our	your (pl)	their	your (polite)
mein	*dein*	*sein*	*ihr*	*sein*	*unser*	*euer*	*ihr*	*Ihr*

	Masculine	Feminine	Neuter	Plural
Nominative	*mein*	*meine*	*mein*	*meine*
Accusative	*meinen*	*meine*	*mein*	*meine*
Genitive	*meines*	*meiner*	*meines*	*meiner*
Dative	*meinem*	*meiner*	*meinem*	*meinen*

Apply the endings of this table for any of the personal pronouns listed on p.218.

2 Declension of articles and adjectives

see Chapter 5: The Definite Article; Chapter 6: The Indefinite Article, and Chapter 28: Adjectival Endings

Definite Article & Group 1 Adjectives

	Masculine	Feminine	Neuter	Plural
Nominative	*der neue Lehrer*	*die neue Lehrerin*	*das schnelle Auto*	*die neuen Häuser*
Accusative	*den neuen Lehrer*	*die neue Lehrerin*	*das schnelle Auto*	*die neuen Häuser*
Genitive	*des neuen Lehrers*	*der neuen Lehrerin*	*des schnellen Autos*	*der neuen Häuser*
Dative	*dem neuen Lehrer*	*der neuen Lehrerin*	*dem schnellen Auto*	*den neuen Häusern*

Like this pattern: *dieser, jener, jeder*

Indefinite Article & Group 2 Adjectives

Nominative	*ein guter Schüler*	*eine gute Studentin*	*ein rotes Auto*	*meine guten Bücher*
Accusative	*einen guten Schüler*	*eine gute Studentin*	*ein rotes Auto*	*meine guten Bücher*
Genitive	*eines guten Schülers*	*einer guten Studentin*	*eines roten Autos*	*meiner guten Bücher*
Dative	*einem guten Schüler*	*einer guten Studentin*	*einem roten Auto*	*meinen guten Büchern*

Like this pattern: *kein, dein, sein, ihr, unser, euer, Ihr*

Group 3 Adjectives

Nominative	*guter Wein*	*frische Milch*	*deutsches Bier*	*leere Gläser*
Accusative	*guten Wein*	*frische Milch*	*deutsches Bier*	*leere Gläser*
Genitive	*guten Weins*	*frischer Milch*	*deutschen Biers*	*leerer Gläser*
Dative	*gutem Wein*	*frischer Milch*	*deutschem Bier*	*leeren Gläsern*

3 Prepositions

Prepositions which take the Accusative case: see Chapter 11

durch	through
ohne	without
gegen	against
wider	against
um	around
für	for
entlang	along

Prepositions which take the Dative case: see Chapter 12

außer	apart from
aus	out
bei	at the house of
mit	with
nach	after; towards
seit	since
von	from
zu	to
gegenüber	opposite

Prepositions which take either the Accusative or Dative case, depending on whether or not movement is implied: see Chapter 13

an	on; at
auf	on
hinter	behind
in	in
neben	next to
über	over
unter	under
vor	in front; ago
zwischen	between

Prepositions which take the Genitive case: see Chapter 14

außerhalb	outside
(an)statt	instead
innerhalb	inside; within
trotz	despite
während	while; during,
wegen	because of

38

RICHTIG ODER FALSCH?
Key to the exercises

Chapter 1
1 Alles in Ordnung?
1. Ich heiße Richard Wagner. 2. Ich bin vierzehn Jahre alt. 3. Wir wohnen in England. 4. Ich habe keine Geschwister. 5. Hamburg liegt in der Nähe von Bremen. 6. Wir haben ein Doppelhaus am Stadtrand. 7. Das kostet zwei Euro. 8. Ich esse mein Frühstück um acht Uhr./ Um acht Uhr esse ich mein Frühstück. 9. Meine Schwester spielt gern Klavier. 10. Das Rathaus liegt in der Stadtmitte./ In der Stadtmitte liegt das Rathaus.

2 Richtig oder falsch?
1. (X) Meine Schwester heißt Monika. 2. ✓ 3. ✓ 4. (X) Ich habe eine Katze. 5. ✓ 6. ✓ 7. (X) Wir haben ein Einfamilienhaus am Stadtrand. 8. ✓ 9. (X) Ich spiele gern Geige. 10. ✓

3 Bildertipps!
Variants possible.
1. Ich wohne in England. 2. Ich spiele gern Trompete. 3. Meine Schlange ist sechs Jahre alt. 4. Wir wohnen in einem Doppelhaus in der Stadtmitte. 5. Mein Auto ist ein Mercedes! 6. Ich lerne gern Mathe. 7. Ich wohne in einer Wohnung. 8. In Wales spricht man Englisch. 9. Eine Kassette kostet sechs Euro fünfzig. 10. Ich esse nicht gern Eier!

Chapter 2
1 Ein Interview. Lückentexte!
1. Wie? 2. Wie viel ? 3. Wie. 4. Was für? 5. Wo/Wann/Um wie viel Uhr? 6. Welche? 7. Wer? 8. Was/Wie viel? 9. Wie? 10. Wann/Um wie viel Uhr?

2 Mischmasch
1. Hast du Haustiere? 2. Wohnst du in der Stadtmitte? 3. Ist das weit von hier? 4. Was isst du zum Abendessen? 5. Kann man direkt fahren? 6. Wollen Sie das bitte wiederholen? 7. Kannst du dein Haus beschreiben? 8. Haben wir jetzt Deutsch? 9. Habt ihr heute Hausaufgaben auf? 10. Seid ihr alle fertig?

Grammatik Aktiv!

3 Wie heißt die Frage?
Variants possible.
1. Hast du Geschwister? 2. Wohnst du in Österreich? 3. Was ist dein Lieblingsfach? 4 Was/Wie viel kostet das? 5. Wo liegt Hamburg/Bremen?

Chapter 3
1 Ordnung muss sein!
1. Hört gut zu! 2. Zeig mir dein Heft! 3. Füllt die Lücken aus! 4. Lies den Text vor! 5. Schreibt die Hausaufgaben auf! 6. Wiederholen Sie bitte die Frage! 7. Arbeitet jetzt in Gruppen! 8. Stelle deinem Partner Fragen! 9. Sprechen Sie bitte langsamer! 10. Entschuldigen Sie bitte meine Verspätung!

2 Bildertipps!
Answers from Exercise 1 are numbered against the letter from Exercise 2.
1c, 2g, 3d, 4b, 5j, 6h, 7a, 8e, 9i, 10f

3 Was passt wozu?
1d, 2g, 3c, 4b, 5f, 6j, 7a, 8i, 9h, 10e

Chapter 4
1 Wo steht das Substantiv?
<u>Unterstrichene</u> Substantive sind:
1. Vater, Rainer, Leiter, Volksbank. 2. Schwester, Bruder. 3. Geburtstag, Dezember, März. 4. Onkel, Auto, Audi, Mercedes. 5. Bodensee, Schweiz, Österreich, Deutschland.

2 Maskulinum oder ...? Singular oder ...?

	SINGULAR (s.)		PLURAL (p.)
Maskulinum (m.)	Femininum (f.)	Neutrum (n.)	
a. Vater, Rainer	Mutter	Auto, Frankreich	Renaults, Autos
b. Bruder, Sohn	Schwester, Sophie, Tochter.	Schottland	Geschwister, Schwestern
c. Mittwoch, Donnerstag	Schule, Erdkunde, Informatik, Woche.	x	Fächer, Lieblingsfächer
d. Sommer, Juli, August	Kellnerin	Hotel, Österreich	Hotels
e. Bruder, Bodensee, (St. Moritz.)	Kusine, Nordsee, Schweiz	Surfen, Pferderennen	Uhren
f. Montag	Schule	x	Busse, Schülern
g. x	x	Wetter	Engländer, Franzosen
h. Herr Schmidt	Frau Müller	x	Postkarten, Vereinigten S.

3 So ein Mist!
Completed words:
Berlin, Dezember, Bruder, Brief, Deutsch, Familie, Schwestern, Ulrike, Sabine, Geschwister, Haustiere, Katze, Goldfische, Winter, Autos, Österreich, Hotels, Salzburg, Hausaufgaben, Bücher, Postkarten, Alpen, Elke.

Chapter 5
1 Der, die oder das?
1. der 2. der/dieser 3. das/dieses 4. die 5. die/diese 6. den 7. diese 8. das 9. die(se) 10. die(se) 11. des 12. der/dieser 13. des 14. der 15. der 16. zu dem/zum 17. der 18. in dem/im 19. der 20. der

2 Der, die, das …? auf jeden Fall …?
1. das, die, der, das, der, des 2. der, der, dem, dem, den, des 3. die, die, das, der, dem 4. die, der, der, des, den

3 Der, die, das? Dieser? Jener? Jeder? Solcher? Welcher…?
1. Welches, dieses , jenes? 2. Jede, der, diese, dem 3. Die, die(se), solche, die 4. Welche, diese, jene 5. Jeden, solche, dem/im

Chapter 6
1 Lückentexte
1. Ein/mein/dein, ein/dein/mein 2. eine 3. ein 4. kein 5. kein 6. kein/ein 7. eine 8. einen, keine 9. eine 10. eine, keine 11. einer 12. eines Lehrers 13. eines Kaninchens 14. eines Bundeslandes 15. eines Tages 16. (m)einer 17. (k)einem 18. einer 19. einem 20. einem

2 Ein Artikel oder kein Artikel?
1. deine, ihr, dein, sein 2. einen, unser, eine, ihr, unsere, meiner, keine 3. deine, meine, meine, *no article, meines 4. unserem, einen, Ihre, Ihren, Ihrem, eine, keinen, Ihrem, *no article 5. ein, unser, euer, unsere, unseres, *no article

Chapter 7
1 Aufschreiben!
a9, b7, c4, d3, e6, f10, g5, h1, i8, j2

2 Alle Zahlen zählen!
1. fünfzehn 2. fünfzehnten Juli 3. zwei 4. neunzehn-sechs-drei 5. einundzwanzig (b) 6. eins, neun, null, sechs, drei **bzw.** neunzehn, null, dreiundsechzig 7. neunzehn Mark neunzig 8. Tausend neunhundertneunundneunzig Mark 9. neunzehnhundertdreiundsechzig 10. anderthalb

3 Schule, Noten, Zeugnisse und Mathe!

einunddreißigsten, sechzehn, zehnten, achthundert, elf, achtzehn, acht, neun Uhr, fünfzehn Uhr dreißig, ersten, zwei Komma null.

Chapter 8

1 Wie spät ist es jetzt in Wien?

1a. vierundzwanzig Uhr/Mitternacht 1b. achtzehn Uhr/sechs Uhr abends
2a. neunzehn Uhr/sieben Uhr abends 2b. sechzehn Uhr/vier Uhr abends
3a. Viertel vor drei 3b. Viertel vor zwölf 4a. halb elf abends 4b. halb sieben morgens
5. zwei Uhr fünfunddreißig (morgens) 5b. siebzehn Uhr fünfunddreißig

2 Den wievielten haben wir heute?

1. Heute haben wir Montag, den ersten Januar. 2. Heute haben wir Mittwoch, den dritten März. 3. Heute haben wir Donnerstag, den einunddreißigsten Mai. 4. Heute haben wir Samstag, den zwölften Oktober. 5. Heute haben wir Dienstag, den achtundzwanzigsten Februar.

3 Früher oder später…!

1f, 2i, 3c, 4e, 5d, 6g, 7a, 8b, 9h

Chapter 9

1 Mehr oder weniger?

1R, 2F, 3F, 4R, 5R, 6R, 7F, 8F, 9R, 10F

2 Ein Apfelkuchen – mein Lieblingsrezept!

dreihundert Gramm Weizenmehl, drei Eier, hundert Milliliter Milch, hundertzwanzig Gramm Butter, fünfhundert Gramm/ein Pfund Äpfel, zehn Gramm Backpulver, hundertsiebzig Gramm Zucker, neunzig Minuten, Durchschnitts temperatur, hundertneunzig Grad Celsius

3 Messen, wiegen, ertmals fragen!

1. Ich bin ein Meter siebzig groß. 2. Sie ist ein Meter fünfundsechzig groß. 3. Ich wiege dreiundsiebzig Kilo. 4. In einer normalen Weinflasche gibt es siebzig Zentiliter (0,70 Liter) Wein. 5. Drei Komma drei Pfund sind anderthalb Kilo. 6. Er ist anderthalb Meter lang. Er ist neunzig Zentimeter breit. Er ist fünfundsechzig Zentimeter hoch. 7. London ist circa fünfhundertfünfzig Kilometer von Bonn entfernt. 8. Im Sommer haben wir zwanzig bis dreißig Grad Celsius.

Chapter 10
1 So ein Durcheinander!
1. Ich habe einen Großvater. Er heißt Thomas. 2. Meine Mutter ist Lehrerin. Sie isst gern Salat. 3. Hast du ein Kaninchen? Mein Kaninchen gefällt mir gut! 4. Meine Eltern haben zwei Autos. Beide Autos sind etwas alt. 5. Meine Brüder beißen niemals meinen Hund. 6. Diesen Montag schreibt mein Brieffreund eine Klassenarbeit.

2 Und noch mehr
Nominative (subject) = underlined; accusative (direct object) = double underlined.
1. Ich habe einen Großvater. Er heißt Thomas. 2. Meine Mutter ist Lehrerin. Sie isst gern Salat. 3. Hast du ein Kaninchen? Mein Kaninchen gefällt mir gut! 4. Meine Eltern haben zwei Autos. Beide Autos sind etwas alt. 5. Meine Brüder beißen niemals meinen Hund. 6. Diesen Montag schreibt mein Brieffreund eine Klassenarbeit.

3 Lücken, Lücken überall
1. der, er 2. den, die, den 3. das, ein, eine, ein 4. es, keine, eine 5. dein, dein 6. es, meine 7. nächstes 8. nächsten, nächste 9. meine, sie, eine, sie

4 Noch mehr Lücken
1. mein, meinen 2. deine, meine 3. das, es 4. das, es, den 5. welche 6. diese

5 Bildertipps!
1. Welche Kartoffeln esst ihr am liebsten? 2. Das Verkehrsamt finden Sie vor dem Dom. 3. Wo ist mein Taschenrechner? 4. Also, diese holländischen Kartoffeln schmecken uns am besten. 5. Entschuldigung! Wo liegt hier bitte das Verkehrsamt? Ist es weit von hier entfernt? 6. Nein! Ist das deine Sporttasche? Ich kann meine Sporttasche nicht finden!

Chapter 11
1 P-zon-loch!
ohne, wider, gegen, um, durch, für/ohne, entlang

2 In Ordnung!
1. Mutti! Kannst du meine Hausaufgaben für mich machen? 2. Wider meines Vaters Willen möchte ich ein Motorrad. 3. Durch Satellit kann ich deutsche Fernsehprogramme bekommen. 4. Heute Abend gehen wir um zwanzig Uhr in die Disko. 5. Am besten fahren Sie die Autobahn entlang nach Berlin. 6. Nimmst du deinen Tee mit oder ohne Milch? 7. Wir haben null zu vier gegen unsere Partnerschule verloren! 8. Tschüs! Bis nächsten Samstag!

3 Stau um Hamburg

bis, entlang, durch, um, ohne, gegen, wider, für, bis

4 Bilder sprechen Bände!

1. Nächstes Jahr fahren wir durch den Kanaltunnel nach Frankreich. 2. Durch Satellit kann ich deutsche Fernsehprogramme bekommen. 3. Letztes Jahr haben wir wider meinen Willen eine Kaffeepause für meine Oma gemacht. 4. Ich fahre niemals auf Urlaub ohne meinen Fotoapparat. 5. Wir haben null zu vier gegen unsere Partnerschule verloren!

Chapter 12
1 Was fehlt?

1. Außer, zu 2. aus 3. von 4. seit 5. seit, gegenüber 6. mit 7. zu, von 8. bei, außer 9. bei 10. zu, gegenüber

2 Dativ – mit oder ohne Präposition?

1. meinem, zum, aus 2. mir, zur 3. bei 4. der 5. dir 6. einem, dem

3 Dativ: jetzt bist du daran!

1. einem, der 2. diesem, dem 3. der, Herrn 4. mir, dir 5. meiner 6. meinen, dem, die

Chapter 13
1 Mischmasch

Variants possible.

1. Wie komme ich am besten zum Verkehrsamt? 2. Die Realschule liegt auf der rechten Seite hinter dem Theater. 3. In meinem Zimmer habe ich eine Kuckucksuhr an der Wand. 4. Lege ich diese Messer auf den Tisch oder kommen sie in die Schublade? 5. Fahren Sie hier geradeaus bis zur Kreuzung. 6. Das Kino finden Sie zwischen dem Eiscafé und der Post. 7. Vor zwei Jahren wohnte ich hinterm Schloss und neben der Stadthalle. 8. Ich möchte etwas über mein Lieblingsthema erzählen.

2 P-zon-loch!

1. auf, auf 2. dem, meine 3. dem, dem 4. ins, im 5. den, die 6. Am, den, an 7. der, im 8. die, im 9. das, dem 10. der, zwischen, den

Chapter 14
1 So ein Mist!

Wegen/infolge, während, trotz, infolge/wegen, außerhalb, jenseits, diesseits, innerhalb, anstatt, jenseits

2 P-zon-loch!

1. der 2. meiner 3. meiner/der 4. meines 5. meiner 6. eines 7. unseres, unserer
8. des, der

Chapter 15
1 Verben und Lücken

1. heißt 2. wohne 3. spielen 4. macht 5. macht 6. studieren 7. wohnt 8. regnet
9. warten 10. spielst

2 Andere Verben, andere Lücken

1. bin 2. hast 3. wird 4. haben 5. sind 6. ist, ist 7. habt 8. hat 9. wird 10. wird

3 Welches Verb? Welche Form?

1C, 2D, 3H, 4A, 5J, 6B, 7I, 8F, 9G, 10E

Chapter 16
1 Was passt wozu?

1J, 2H, 3E, 4I, 5C, 6G, 7A, 8F, 9D, 10B

2 Was fehlt?

1. fahren 2. siehst 3. lesen 4. tragen 5. spricht 6. liest 7. essen 8. trägt 9. sehen
10. fährt

3 Lückentext

1. beginnt 2. gibt 3. hältst 4. hilfst 5. nimmst 6. schlafen 7. seid 8. wäscht 9. weißt
10. empfehlen

4 Bildertipps

1. Wir essen gern italienisch. 2. Wie oft spielst du Karten? 3. Das Wetter ist jetzt
schöner: es wird endlich sonnig! 4. Wir haben Winterferien Ende Februar. Sie sind
ideal zum Skifahren. Und du? 5. Was trägst du meistens am Wochenende? Ich
trage gern ein T-Shirt und eine Jeans.

Chapter 17
1 Wie spielt man 'Rugby'?

1. darf 2. sollen 3. kann 4. dürfen 5. müssen 6. soll 7. will 8. dürfen 9. mag

2 Jens im Unglück

a. soll b. mag c. will/wollte d. musst e. darf f. kannst

3 Was darfst du tun?

1. dürfen 2. will 3. sollst 4. wollen 5. muss 6. könnte

Grammatik Aktiv!

4 Was ist die Lösung?

1h, 2a, 3f, 4e, 5c, 6b, 7d, 8g

5 E-Mail aus Deutschland

1. Du sollst auch deinen Bruder von mir grüßen. 2. Ihr solltet diese CD anhören. 3. Vielleicht kann ich dann die CD kaufen. 4. Ich möchte einen Computer zum Geburtstag. 5. Was willst du zum Geburtstag? 6. Mein Onkel Frank und seine Frau wollen nach Kanada auswandern. 7. Meine Kusinen können beide schon sehr gut Französisch. 8. Jetzt müssen sie auch Englisch lernen. 9. Um wie viel Uhr musst du ins Bett gehen? 10. Ich darf bis 10.30 Uhr abends wach bleiben. 11. Das ist alles, was ich dir zur Zeit erzählen kann.

Chapter 18

1 Wechseln, bitte!

1. ich werde kommen. 2. wir werden singen 3. du wirst schlafen 4. Sie werden sehen 5. er wird lernen. 6. Wir werden einkaufen gehen. 7. Ich werde meine Hausaufgaben machen. 8. Markus und seine Schwester werden ihren Opa besuchen. 9. Petra wird in ihrem Zimmer fernsehen. 10. Werdet ihr mitkommen?

2 Wie sieht die Zukunft aus?

1. Ich werde mein Abitur machen. 2. Ich werde meinen Zivildienst ableisten. 3. Ich werde dann Englisch an der Universität studieren. 4. Ich werde eine Stelle finden. 5. Ich werde eine schöne Frau heiraten. 6. Meine Frau und ich werden viele Kinder bekommen.

3 Ab in die Sonne

1. werden 2. wird 3. werde 4. wird 5. wirst 6. werden, werden

4 Pläne, planen

1. Oma wird einen Pulli stricken. 2. Stefan wird Tennis spielen. 3. Herr Graf wird eine Zeitung lesen. 4. Sandra und Gerd werden ins Kino gehen. 5. Tante Petra wird im Garten arbeiten. 6. Ich werde einen Brief schreiben.

Chapter 19

1 Was haben sie heute Morgen gemacht?

1. Ich habe mir die Zähne geputzt. 2. Herr Reuter ist mit dem Zug gefahren *or* angekommen. 3. Wir haben Tischtennis gespielt. 4. Du bist im Schwimmbad geschwommen. 5. Charley und Lisbeth haben den Tisch abgeräumt.

2 Am Wochenende

1. aufgestanden 2. gegessen 3. gespielt 4. gegangen 5. eingeschlafen

3 Ich habe schon alles gemacht

1. Was hast du gedacht? 2. Wir haben dir geholfen. 3. Er hat 20,-DM gefunden.
4. Haben Sie es gewusst? 5. Das habe ich gewusst. 6. Ich bin nach Hause
gekommen. 7. Sie hat bis 10 Uhr geschlafen. 8. Wir sind im Kino gewesen.
9. Er hat im Krankenhaus gelegen. 10. Er hat in Berlin gewohnt.

4 Das fünfte Rad

(Sentences are examples only – reason for the odd-one-out status is given in
brackets)

1. gelaufen (auxiliary = sein)	Micha ist dreißig Kilometer gelaufen.
2. vergessen (only irregular)	Ich habe meinen Regenschirm vergessen.
3. genommen (auxiliary = haben)	Haben Sie diesen Stift genommen?
4. gesehen (only irregular)	Man hat sie gestern gesehen.
5. gemacht (only regular)	Wir haben eine schöne Radtour gemacht.

Chapter 20
1 Was sagen sie?

1. uns 2. dich 3. mich 4. sich 5. uns 6. mir 7. sich

2 Fragen und Antworten

1. Ich freue mich auf meinen Geburtstag. 2. Wir kennen uns seit zwei Jahren. 3. Ich
interessiere mich für Kunst. 4. Wir treffen uns vor dem Kino. 5. Es befindet sich in
der Klarastraße.

3 Wie mein Tag anfängt

stehe ich auf / rasiert sich / dusche ich mich / ziehe ich mich an / setze ich mich /
esse / verlasse / entscheide ich mich / bin ich

Chapter 21
1 Aussteigen – steigen aus

1. Ich steige am Hauptbahnhof aus. 2. Der Zug fährt um 14.27 Uhr ab. 3. Wir
fangen unsere Hausaufgaben an. 4. Erzählst du bitte deine Geschichte weiter?
5. Die Lehrerin sagt: 'Ihr lest das Gedicht vor.'

2 Die Qual der Wahl

1. Die Studenten wiederholen den Satz. 2. Ute steigt in Köln um. 3. Thomas fährt
hin. 4. Übersetzen Sie ins Englische, bitte schön! 5. Ich hoffe, wir sehen uns bald
wieder.

Chapter 22
1 Suchrätsel

M	I	H	R	B	D	Y	I	H	N
I	A	P	B	Q	H	T	G	M	Y
C	S	I	C	H	N	D	K	I	I
H	S	I	E	D	E	E	L	R	H
M	J	Z	X	I	N	S	P	V	M
I	B	E	A	C	P	W	Y	M	J
H	D	P	L	H	J	G	F	S	Q
R	I	U	W	I	R	W	Z	D	U
K	R	N	X	A	U	E	U	C	H
T	F	S	I	H	E	R	M	N	O

Antwort: IHNEN

2 Frohe Weinachten
Suggested answers.
2. Ich schenke Opa eine Flasche Whisky. Ich schenke sie ihm. 3. Ich schenke Mutti einen Schal. Ich schenke ihn ihr. 4. Ich schenke Oma Socken. Ich schenke sie ihr.
5. Ich schenke der Mietze ein Gummimäuschen. Ich schenke es ihr. 6. Ich schenke Vater einen Reiseatlas. Ich schenke ihn ihm. 7. Ich schenke Tante Dora eine Wärmflasche. Ich schenke sie ihr.

3 Bericht eines Besuches
Er, mir, Ich, ihn, ich, ihm, Ich, ihm, Er, ich, ihn, Sie, ich, ihr, Sie, uns, sie, Ich, sie Sie, sie, mich, ich, mich.

Chapter 23
1 Wann – wie – wo?
1. Ich fahre jeden Tag mit dem Bus zur Schule. 2. Mein Austauschpartner ist gestern Abend aus Frankreich angekommen. 3. Hast du Lust, morgen zu einem Fußballspiel zu gehen? 4. Steffi soll ihren Freund um sechs Uhr vor dem Stadttheater treffen. 5. Vater arbeitet bis acht Uhr im Büro. 6. Wir mussten gestern wegen schlechten Wetters zu Hause bleiben.

Chapter 24
1 In Ordnung?
1. Rotwein gefällt mir nicht. 2. Warst du niemals in Österreich? 3. Ich habe keine Geschwister. 4. Wir haben nichts zu verzollen. 5. Habt ihr keine Hausaufgaben gemacht? 6. Handelt niemals mit Drogen! 7. Ich habe gestern nichts geschrieben. 8. Ich kann mein Geld nirgendwo finden. 9. Will keiner uns helfen? 10. Ich habe kein Wort verstanden.

2 Was passt wozu?
1e, 2b, 3c, 4f, 5d, 6a.

Chapter 25
1 Alles über Claudia
1. Mein Bruder isst gern Erdbeeren, aber ich esse lieber Himbeeren. 2. Jeden Tag übe ich Flöte, bevor ich zur Schule gehe. 3. Unsere Lehrer sind böse auf uns, weil wir unsere Hausaufgaben nicht gemacht haben. 4. Ich treffe meinen Freund, wenn wir in die Stadt gehen. 5. Hast du gehört, dass ich einen Kunstpreis gewonnen habe?

2 Alles über Kai
1. obwohl 2. und 3. dass 4. wenn 5. weil 6. bevor

Chapter 26
1 Lebensmittel vom Supermarkt
1. die 2. den 3. deren 4. denen 5. das

2 Ein Ding, das …
1. Ein Flugzeug ist eine Maschine, die fliegen kann. 2. Herr Weichmantel ist ein Mann, der einen Bart trägt. 3. Ein Eisbär ist ein Tier, das ein weißes Fell hat. 4. Ich lese ein Buch, das sehr interessant ist. 5. Ein Porsche ist ein Wagen, der sehr schnell fährt. 6. Ein Wolkenkratzer ist ein Gebäude, das viele Stockwerke hat.

3 Ich kenne eine Person
1. die 2. der 3. den 4. das 5. das 6. dem 7. deren 8. der 9. dessen 10. der

Chapter 27
1 Die Steigerungsformen
1. kälter 2. älter 3. schneller 4. teu(e)rer 5. kleiner 6. größer

2. Die Steigerungsformen II
1. größer 2. schön 3. wichtig 4. interessantesten 5. höchsten 6. jung / jüngsten 7. gut / besser 8. früher / am frühsten

Grammatik Aktiv!

3 Wer ist der Beste?

1. schneller 2. besser 3. ist grösser als 4. alt wie Michas (Katze). 5. war es kälter als heute.

4 Liebe Geschwister

	Julia	Roland	Georg
Alter:			1. ist das älteste Kind
Tennis spielen:	2. spielt am besten		
Größe:	3. ist das größte Kind	4. ist kleiner als Georg	
Fremdsprachen:	5. spricht am besten Englisch		
Singen:		6. singt am liebsten	

Chapter 28
1 Ganz im Gegenteil

1. langweiliges 2. jüngeren 3. schlechten 4. weißen 5. neuen 6. schnelle

2 Weihnachtswünsche

1. ein schnelles Fahrrad 2. einen guten Fußball 3. einen tollen Computer 4. ein schwarzes Paar Schuhe 5. eine moderne Stereo-Anlage 6. einen bunten Papagei 7. ein blaues Hemd 8. eine neue Jeans-Hose

3 Was ich zur Zeit lese

Letzte Woche las ich ein ganz <u>interessantes</u> Buch. Es war ein <u>spannender</u> Roman. Der <u>junge</u> Held und seine <u>hübsche</u> Partnerin fuhren nach Deutschland. Sie mussten eine <u>gefährliche</u> Mission durchführen. Sie flogen nach Berlin in einem <u>großen</u> Flugzeug. Dort haben sie einen <u>fremden</u> Agenten kennengelernt, der ihnen <u>wichtige</u> Pläne verkauft hatte. Sie brachten die <u>teueren</u> Pläne zum Hauptquartier des <u>britischen</u> Geheimdiensts zurück. Am Ende dieser <u>großartigen</u> Geschichte hat der Held sich in seine <u>junge</u> Partnerin verliebt, was mir gar nicht gefiel!

Chapter 29
1 Erinnerungen an die Sommerferien

war, besuchte, war, wohnte, hatte, ging, hieß, hatte, nahm, fuhr, sah, durfte, aßen, kehrten, schlief, hatte, teilte, lebte, starb, war, hatten, freute, fuhr

2 Im Polizierevier

1. Sie besuchte ihre Schwester in Berlin. 2. Sie fuhren in Österreich Ski. 3. Sie war ganz faul – sie machte nichts. 4. Sie schlief das ganze Wochenende lang. 5. Freunde feierten mit ihr ihren Geburtstag. 6. Sie sah fern. 7. Sie brach in ein großes Haus ein.

3 Was stimmt: 1, 2 oder 3?

1. he had to 2. we slept 3. you came 4. you sat 5. I read 6. sie hörten 7. ich wollte
8. wir fragten 9. Sie sahen 10. er spielte

4 Wann passierte das?

1. entdeckte 2. begann 3. starb 4. endete 5. landete 6. feierten

Chapter 30
1 Schlagzeilen

1. werden 2. wird 3. wurden 4. sind, worden 5. wird

2 Die Verwandlung

1. Ein berüchtiger Dieb ist am Dienstag verhaftet worden. 2. Die Oskars für dieses
Jahr wurden letzten Dienstag verliehen. 3. Die Arbeit wird bitte mit größter
Sorgfältigkeit geschrieben. 4. Fisch wird immer Freitags gegessen. 5. Das nächste
Konzert des Berliner Stadtorchesters ist abgesagt worden.

Chapter 31
1 Wenn es nur so leicht wäre

1e, 2d, 3h, 4a, 5f, 6b, 7c, 8g

2 Kurz und bündig

sei, handele, verbinde; sei, wolle, vermute, gehe, seien, wäre; sei, hätten, sei, sei,
könnte

Chapter 32
1 Paare

1c, 2d, 3a, 4e, 5b

2 Gestern

1. Frau Springs hatte eine Zeitung im Café gelesen. 2. Angela und Petra hatten
Squash im Fitness-Zentrum gespielt. 3. Roland hatte einen Aufsatz in der Schule
geschrieben. 4. Herr Beckmann hatte Blumen für seine Frau gekauft. 5. Christoph
war mit dem Zug von Bremen gefahren.

3 Das gehört nicht dazu

1. hattet > hatte 2. hatte > war, gefahrt > gefahren 3. warst > waren 4. gewinnen >
gewonnen 5. hatten > hatte 6. bekommt > bekommen 7. *no incorrect forms* 8. war >
hatte

Grammatik Aktiv!

Chapter 33
1 Was fehlt?
1. Ich heiße Uwe. Mein Haus liegt in Wien. 2. Wie gefällt dir dieser Rotwein?
3. Könnten Sie mir bitte die Speisekarte reichen? 4. Als meine Frau viel jünger
war, hieß sie Fräulein Bäcker. Jetzt heißt sie Frau Müller. 5. Ulli! Du musst mir
helfen! Alle Wände meiner Häuser müssen wir renovieren. 6. Ich bin älter als
du: könntest du bitte auf die Leiter steigen?

2 Wie schreibt man das?
1. Wie heißt du? 2. Mein Haus liegt zwischen Wien und Salzburg. 3. Ich wohne in
der Nähe von der Schweiz. 4. Als ich jünger war, musste ich viel schreiben.
5. Wir reisen lieber mit dem Flugzeug nach Deutschland als mit dem Zug.

Chapter 34
1 Ein totales Durcheinander!

Köln, den 24. März 1999.

Sehr geehrter Herr Thompson!

Ich bedanke mich herzlich für Ihren Brief, der uns gestern erreicht hat. Wenn ich
Sie richtig verstehe, möchten Sie und Ihre Kollegen unser Büro am 30. März
besuchen. Ich glaube leider nicht, dass wir Sie diesmal begrüßen können, weil
unsere Fabrik geschlossen ist. Ich möchte Ihnen aber folgenden Vorschlag machen:
Kommen Sie doch selber mit Ihrer Frau bzw. ihrer Sekretärin. Wenn Sie Zeit
hätten, könnte ich Ihnen meine Stadt zeigen. Was meinen Sie dazu?

Den Rhein und seinen Wein müssen Sie doch näher kennen lernen.

Ich wünsche Ihnen eine gute Reise und viel Spaß in Köln !

Mit freundlichen Grüßen,
Müller.

2 Wörterbuchübung!
betrifft, eventuellen, siebten Mai, zweitausendeins, zweiten Mai, dreißigsten April,
siebten des Monats, zur Zeit, circa, sechseinhalb Millionen Euro, beziehungsweise,
unter anderem, gegebenenfalls, im Auftrag

Chapter 35
1 Das ist neu!
A. 2. Tipp 4. Kunststoffflasche 6. muss 8. heißen 9. müsst 10. verlässt
B. 2. Rad fahren 4. spazieren gehen 5. kennen lernen 7. rot gestreift 8. hart gekocht
9. wie viel ?
C. 2. gestern Abend 3. im Allgemeinen 6. auf Deutsch 8. das schwarze Brett
10. jedes Mal.
D. 2. Photographie/ Fotografie 3. Telephon/ Telefon 4. Delphin/ Delfin
5. Ketschup 7. Jogurt 8. Känguru